BONHOEFFER

A *Brief Overview*
of the Life and Writings of
Dietrich Bonhoeffer

1906-1945

JOHN W. MATTHEWS

Lutheran University Press
Minneapolis, Minnesota

BONHOEFFER

A *Brief Overview of the*
Life and Writings of Dietrich Bonhoeffer
1906-1945
by John W. Matthews
Albert Anderson, Theology for Life Series editor

Cover and interior design: Karen Walhof

Library of Congress Cataloging-in-Publication Data

Matthews, John W., 1949-
  Bonhoeffer : a brief overview of the life and writings of
Dietrich Bonhoeffer, 1906-1945 / by John W. Matthews.
      p. cm. — (Theology for life series)
  Includes bibliographical references (p. 88).
  ISBN-13: 978-1-932688-65-8 (alk. paper)
  ISBN-10: 1-932688-65-X (alk. paper)
  1. Bonhoeffer, Dietrich, 1906-1945. I. Title.
  BX4827.B57M372 2011
  230'.044092—dc23
  [B]
                                    2011039079

Lutheran University Press, PO Box 390759, Minneapolis, MN 55439
www.lutheranupress.org
Manufactured in the United States of America

Table of Contents

Eberhard Bethge with Dietrich Bonhoeffer, 1938

Dedication

To Larry Pratt
my pastor, mentor, and friend

Foreword

"Don't give the plot away by revealing the end!" is a rule that conscientious critics impose upon themselves. Reviewers of *Bonhoeffer* by John Matthews need not follow such a rule because the author himself gives his plot away by boldly revealing the end and beginning of his book on page 1. He frames the life-long, or at least vocation-long, focus of theologian Dietrich Bonhoeffer around the theme of Christology, which appeared in the title of the first English translation, *Christ the Center.* Christ was at the beginning, middle, and end of Bonhoeffer's life work. What pastors Bonhoeffer and Matthews do with that theme is what makes this book so cogent, concentrated, and clear.

Matthews also frames this Christological focus around the chronology of Bonhoeffer and the Germany of his time. The Christology lectures date from 1933, when Adolf Hitler came to power and the references continue to Bonhoeffer's last letters as Hitler's prisoner. He was executed in 1945, the same spring that saw the death of Hitler. In the prison letters, Bonhoeffer asked Bethge, "Who is Christ actually for us today?" Matthews says this question is rhetorical, because Bonhoeffer intended for it to stimulate deeper reflection. Bonhoeffer's friend and biographer Eberhard Bethge saw 1933, when his subject was only twenty-seven years old, as "the high point of Bonhoeffer's academic career," because it was in that year he delivered the Christology lectures.

A reader new to Bonhoeffer might wonder why Matthews is so taken with Bonhoeffer's Christology and so eager to get readers to share the focus. Some of the reasons have to do with side issues in the Bonhoeffer biography, while others are central. In an earlier book, Matthews took his title from a Bonhoeffer passage that dealt with some radical and deeply rooted themes. Perhaps because Matthews is a pastor, he is close to people who are anxious about their faith, and who may, while reading Bonhoeffer, at first experience some anxiety. "Who is Christ actually for [them] today?"

There is a somewhat polemical tinge to Matthews' treatment, a concern which many of us have reason to share. He does not need to elaborate, but he does specify what is at stake. Instead of facing Jesus in the "suffering God," the "hidden God," popular culture manifests our fascination with the figure of Jesus of Nazareth within the mists of "spirituality," far from the concrete community and world in which Jesus has chosen to be revealed. Not that Bonhoeffer himself was not interested in "Jesus" and "spirituality." He wrote some of the great spiritual works of his century. Books like *Discipleship* continue to serve readers who reckon with Jesus. Yet Matthews knows how easy it is to take this human Jesus captive and find him too weak to speak to the suffering heart or world.

To suggest why this emphasis on Christ and Christology is valuable, even urgent, in the life of faith, here's a story. My wife and I annually find ourselves in the company of friends who could best be described as "religio-secular-spiritual." Highlights of those relationships are our three-hour meals, with convivial but often deep conversations. One year "Jesus" was a popular topic among the New Age crowd, and all twenty of us spoke up. At one point the host posed a question: "Everyone here likes Jesus, but it sounds so different when xxx and xxx talk about him than when yyy and yyy do. How do you account for that?" His son-in-law said, respectfully, "It's really very simple, Dad. Half the people at the table think that Jesus was a very nice guy; the other half think he's the risen Lord."

That distinction need not lead to exclusivity, distancing, or pride by one set of diners or the other. But as one reads Matthews, it is clear that in Bonhoeffer's case "Christ the center" colors everything. Merely affirming that is not a cure-all for life's problems or an answer to all theological questions. Matthews points to many of its limits and points to some answers to the question, "Who is Christ actually for us today?"

In short compass, this book takes up numerous corollary and a few tangential questions. The author deals with issues that have risen in the three-score years after the Holocaust, such as Bonhoeffer's attitude towards Jews. Matthews raises questions about some of Bonhoeffer's claims, for example, that "the world has come of age," and questioning the future of religion itself. Bonhoeffer's works have been published in sixteen translated volumes. It is impossible to deal with all the excitement and problems one finds in his writings and his life. Many of these issues are marginal. But by focusing on Christ the center, Matthews shows what made Bonhoeffer's life cohere. His choices, including his involvement in the plot to kill Hitler, make sense.

In the first paragraph of this foreword I referred to both Bonhoeffer and Matthews as pastors. That linkage was intentional, and it emphasizes what draws me to them. In his short life, Bonhoeffer pursued his vocation in many guises, roles, and offices. In a more serene period than his (what years can match 1933 to 1945 for turbulence?), he may have been simply Professor Bonhoeffer. He could be described, as many have, with words like "teacher," "ecumenical leader," and more. But he was also a pastor, a shepherd to young confir-mands, to grieving seniors, and to comrades in dissent as they faced execution.

Pastor Matthews has impressed me not only for his ability to produce first-rate professorial or academic work, but also for his ability to let his own experience as a pastor color that work. I learned of his academic finesse several years ago when I needed help with the concept of *Disciplina Arcani,* the "discipline of the secret." He saved me from embarrassment and pointed me to an article he had written on the subject. In a time of hyper-individualism in which Jesus is merely a good guy teacher to so many, Matthews as a pastor stresses one of my own favorite Bonhoeffer themes—that Jesus Christ "exists as community." He has discoveries to pass on both to "anxious souls" and to those who move freely, unencumbered by guilt or anxiety through their relation to "Christ the center."

Martin E. Marty
Fairfax M. Cone Distinguished Service
Professor Emeritus at the University of Chicago

Introduction

Dietrich Bonhoeffer's life spanned four decades of the early twentieth century and was shaped within the crucible of two European wars and an economic depression. Born in 1906 and raised in an upper middle class German family, he was educated to be a pastor, further trained as a theologian, involved in a plot to assassinate Adolf Hitler, and finally hanged by the Nazis only days before the end of World War II. But his life story is more than just another tragic episode in the history and horrors of the Holocaust. His was also a life filled with great blessing, even when it required great courage and incredible sacrifice. His relationships were life giving, and his experiences were rich. The authenticity of Bonhoeffer's Christian faith and the integrity of his theology continue to inspire. During that time when most people struggled to protect their own lives and the lives of those they loved, he ventured by faith into uncertain territory, risking his reputation and life to advocate for others. Rarely does one encounter an individual whose inner convictions and outward actions so consistently and courageously match up.

So just what inspired this gifted individual from a prominent family of agnostic intellectuals to prepare for Christian ministry? Why did this young man, raised in Germany during a time between two great wars, seriously consider Christian pacifism? How was it that a person so obedient to the call and command of Jesus Christ could fall in with would-be assassins? And to whom was he answering by ending up a traitor, challenging loyalty and traditional patriotism? These questions, and many more, come to the surface as we engage the life and legacy of Dietrich Bonhoeffer.

The chapters of this book are arranged chronologically in order to observe how Bonhoeffer's beliefs evolve as his life unfolds. Following "A Brief Biography," we will journey with him through his early years of academic preparation, during his active ministry of teaching and preaching, as he serves in military intelligence, and finally in the prison cell where he spent his final days. We are most fortunate that many of his writings were preserved. This book highlights portions of his five major works: *The Communion of Saints, Discipleship, Life Together, Ethics,* and *Letters and Papers from Prison.* Throughout the book, we will see the reasons for his enduring legacy and take note of the challenging issues he raised.

Bonhoeffer was intellectually gifted, and some of his writings and reflections are rather challenging. This book, an introduction to Bonhoeffer and this theology, is an attempt to reveal the blessings found within the life and legacy of this twentieth-century martyr for Jesus Christ. His was a life worthy of respect and emulation.

With the investment of some energy, the reader will find that the words and witness of Dietrich Bonhoeffer have the power to open the heart, enlighten the mind, and inspire the soul.

A Brief Biography

Dietrich Bonhoeffer was born in Breslau, Germany, on February 4, 1906. At the time his father, Dr. Karl Bonhoeffer, was directing the psychiatric department of the Charité Hospital in Breslau (now Wrocław, Poland). His mother, Paula, was the daughter of Karl Alfred von Hase, a professor of practical theology at the university in Breslau, and the granddaughter of famed church historian Karl August von Hase. Karl and Paula Bonhoeffer had eight children: Karl-Friedrich, Walter, Klaus, Ursula, Christine, Dietrich and Sabine (who were twins), and Susanne.

In 1912, Professor Karl Bonhoeffer was appointed chair of the Department of Psychiatry and Neurology at Kaiser Wilhelm University in Berlin. After accepting the position, he moved his family to the Bellevue district and then to the Grünewald neighborhood of Berlin, where they befriended many of the local academics. While Karl instilled in his children a desire for intellectual pursuits, Paula was the one who nurtured them at home. Dietrich, like his siblings, learned traditional German values, Christian piety, scientific curiosity, and an altruistic ethical orientation. While his brothers resonated with their father's cautious agnosticism, Dietrich found himself drawn, like his mother, to religion. His mother's interest in religion had been inspired, in part, by the strong faith she witnessed in the family's Moravian governesses. To his father's surprise, and perhaps chagrin, Dietrich decided to study Hebrew and began pursuing a career in the church. At least part of his decision came from his desire to excel amid a family of high achievers.

After completing his secondary education in 1923 in Berlin, Dietrich began university studies at Tübingen, his father's alma mater. He transferred the following year back to Berlin to study with some of the greatest liberal minds of the early twentieth century: Adolf von Harnack, Hans Lietzmann, Reinhold Seeberg, Karl Holl, and Adolf Diessmann. His vast potential became evident when he completed his doctoral studies in 1927 at the age of twenty-one. His dissertation, entitled "The Communion of Saints," remains to this day a brilliant contribution to Christian theology, combining ecclesiology and sociology in a new, yet fundamental way. He also completed a second dissertation, entitled "Act and Being," which was more philosophical in its focus.

With his academic credentials now in order, Bonhoeffer had to decide between the academic podium and the church pulpit. Partly to qualify for ministry, and partly to give himself time for reflection, he chose to spend the year of 1928 as an assistant pastor in Barcelona, Spain, at a German-speaking congregation. He thoroughly enjoyed his work there, especially with the congregation's pastor, Fritz Olbricht, who Bonhoeffer described as "a man who prefers a good glass of wine, and a good cigar, to a bad sermon."[1]

After returning from Barcelona in February 1929, Bonhoeffer became an academic assistant to Professor Wilhelm Lütgert at Berlin's Kaiser Wilhelm University, and by mid-summer 1930 he was qualified to be a university professor. He was given the opportunity to study at Union Theological Seminary in New York City. It was there that he experienced American enthusiasm for the "social gospel," witnessed the fundamentalist reaction to liberal Christianity, and experienced the fervor of African-American spirituality. He visited the Abyssinian Baptist Church of Harlem with a black classmate named Frank Fisher. Around the same time a French exchange student, Jean Lasserre, introduced him to Christian pacifism. Although he thought that the theology taught at

Union Seminary was more superficial than what he experienced in his native Germany, he was intrigued by his exposure to white and black America during the early years of the Great Depression. Undoubtedly, his encounter with American racism shaped his beliefs about Nazism racism.

On November 15, 1931, in St. Matthias Kirche in Berlin, Dietrich Bonhoeffer was ordained into the Lutheran ministry. While teaching theology at the university, he was also a chaplain to students at the technical university and taught confirmation classes in the lower-class Wedding neighborhood of Berlin. It was at this time that Bonhoeffer became involved in the ecumenical movement. In September 1931, he was appointed youth secretary of the World Alliance Conference in Cambridge.

On January 30, 1933, Adolf Hitler was appointed Reich Chancellor by President Paul von Hindenburg. This appointment was intended to bring unity and focus to a country in the grips of political turmoil, economic and psychological depression, growing unemployment, and overall unrest. Who, at this time, could have imagined the destruction and horror to come with Hitler's "ideology of death"?

The Bonhoeffer family did, and it became apparent to Dietrich Bonhoeffer that such a vision could lead to the genocidal elimination of all peoples not in total conformity with the will of the messianic leader. Aryan legislation, the boycotting of Jewish businesses, and the creation of "enabling laws" proved what the Bonhoeffer family had feared. By fall 1933, Bonhoeffer was collaborating with Martin Niemöller, the outspoken pastor of Berlin-Dahlem, in the formation of the Pastors' Emergency League. Two thousand pastors (Lutheran, Reformed, and United) immediately responded, and their numbers later grew to over seven thousand. Their goal was to resist the encroachment of the new government in all aspects of German life, not least of all the churches.

In large part because of Bonhoeffer's growing opposition to the National Socialist takeover of country, culture, and church, he was given the opportunity to serve two German-speaking congregations in London in October 1933. He ministered there until 1935, all the while soliciting support for German resistance to the Reich. The two churches Bonhoeffer served during this time were the Reformed congregation of St. Paul's (Whitechapel) and the United congregation of Sydenham (South London). While he was still in England, the first Confessing Church assembly was held in Barmen-Wuppertal in May 1934. The Confessing Church (*"Bekennende Kirche"*) evolved out of the Pastors' Emergency League, and it brought together those pastors and laity who opposed the Nazi takeover of the German Evangelical Church by the Nazis as contrary to the essence and expression of the true church. The Barmen Declaration, which came out of that assembly, established the foundation for a new, "illegal," anti-Nazi church. Karl Barth was the primary author of the declaration, and Bonhoeffer was in basic, though not complete, agreement with its content. Later, he would become critical of the Confessing Church for being too concerned about its own institutional existence and not concerned enough to advocate against Nazi abuses. The Barman Declaration did not include any reference to Jews or other persecuted groups.

The Confessing Church's second assembly in 1934 created preacher seminaries to train pastors who would serve congregations which were opposed to the Reich Church and its bishop. Bonhoeffer was called back from England in April 1935 to lead one of these five new seminaries. From its first class of twenty-three ordinands, the Finkenwalde Preacher's Seminary in Pomerania held five courses and trained 149 candidates before the Gestapo closed it in October 1937. It was here that Bonhoeffer's deep friendship with Eberhard Bethge began, a friendship that would last throughout Bonhoeffer's imprisonment and until his death. Bethge became Bonhoeffer's assistant at the seminary, his co-director of later collective pastorates, and finally his biographer. The months of directing the illegal Preachers' Seminary at Finkenwalde also saw Bonhoeffer leading students on visits to Scandinavia, attending ecumenical conferences, and making regular visits to his home in Berlin. By the fall of 1937, because of his well-known opposition to the Nazi regime, he was no longer allowed to teach in Berlin, and the seminary at Finkenwalde was closed. In November 1937, Bonhoeffer's *Discipleship* was published, and the collective pastorates of Kösslin and Gross Schlönwitz were established.

In 1938 Bonhoeffer began speaking with Admiral Canaris, General Beck, and Colonel Hans Oster about the organized opposition to Hitler. Two years later Bonhoeffer was employed by military intelligence and was actively resisting Hitler. Also in 1938, Bonhoeffer assisted his twin sister, Sabine, who was married to Gerhard Leibholz (a Jew who converted to Christianity), in moving her family to England.

In many respects 1939 was a transitional year for Bonhoeffer. His travel to England allowed him to meet George Bell, bishop of Chichester, to whom he spoke about the growing opposition to Hitler.

Still unsure of his own role in Germany's uncertain future, Bonhoeffer accepted an invitation to come to America. On June 2, he departed Berlin, made a brief stop in London, and then traveled across the Atlantic to New York City. After being in America less than a month, he wrote to Reinhold Niebuhr at Union Seminary:

> I have made a mistake in coming to America. I must live through this difficult period of our national history with the Christian people of Germany. I will have no right to participate in the reconstruction of Christian life in Germany after the war if I do not share the trials of this time with my people. . . .

Christians in Germany will face the terrible alternative of either willing the defeat of their nation in
order that Christian civilization may survive, or
willing the victory of their nation and thereby de-
stroying our civilization. I know which of these
alternatives I must choose; but I cannot make that
choice in security.[2]

By July 27 he was back in Berlin, resolved to live in
solidarity with his fellow Germans into an uncertain and
threatening future.

In 1940 Dietrich Bonhoeffer began working in the *Abwehr*,
a military counter-intelligence organization, with Colonel Hans
Oster. Bonhoeffer became associated with the group through
his brother-in-law, Hans von Dohnanyi, who was employed by
the Ministry of Justice and was already working closely with
military counter-intelligence. To keep Bonhoeffer as far away
from the Nazi bureaucracy in Berlin as possible, they had him
assigned to the Munich office. While there, he often visited the
beautiful Benedictine monastery at Ettal and spent significant
time in the winter of 1940-41 writing portions of his book,
Ethics. Although he never completed the work, he considered it
his most important theological project.

Bonhoeffer spent a great deal of time in 1941 and 1942
traveling to Switzerland and Scandinavia, speaking with
persons with whom he could share the plans for opposition to,
and eventual assassination of, Adolf Hitler, thus ending the
Reich. This period was what Bethge has called Bonhoeffer's
"double life." While officially employed by military intelligence,
in fact he was working for the overthrow of the National
Socialists. In October 1941, using *Abwehr* cover, Bonhoeffer
and von Dohnanyi helped fourteen Jews leave Germany through
Switzerland in what became known as Operation Seven.

On January 17, 1943, Dietrich Bonhoeffer became engaged
to Maria von Wedemeyer. Although Bonhoeffer often discouraged others from getting married, since such a commitment

would restrict one's ability to be fully dedicated to important church matters and inevitably place others at risk, his heart overruled his head and his engagement to Maria was sealed just three months before he was imprisoned. On April 5, Dietrich Bonhoeffer was arrested at his parents' home in Berlin-Charlottenburg and taken to Tegel Military Prison in northwest Berlin, where he remained until September 1944.

While in Tegel Prison, Bonhoeffer was allowed family visitors, including his fiancée, Maria. During his time in prison, he wrote *Letters and Papers from Prison*, in addition to a drama and novel, which were later published as *Fiction from Tegel Prison,* which is volume seven of the *Dietrich Bonhoeffer Works.*[3] Although he hoped he would be released during the first year and a half of imprisonment, the Gestapo's discovery of *Abwehr* files that contained incriminating evidence caused him to be transferred to the maximum-security prison at the Gestapo headquarters in Berlin. From this time on, Bonhoeffer had little contact with his family, and his hope for release began to evaporate. He abandoned a plan for escape in early October 1944, because it would have put his brother, Klaus, and his brothers-in-law, Hans and Rüdiger, at risk.

On February 7, 1945, Bonhoeffer was taken to Buchenwald, later to Regensburg, then to Schönberg, and eventually to Flossenbürg, where he was executed the morning of April 9. Along with Bonhoeffer, Colonel Hans Oster, Admiral Wilhelm Canaris, Dr. Karl Sack, Captain Ludwig Gehre, and Roland Strünck were hanged in one of Hitler's last desperate acts of retribution against those accused of undermining his Third Reich. On the same day, Bonhoeffer's brother-in-law, Hans von Dohnanyi, was executed in Sachsenhausen, and two weeks later, his brother, Klaus, and brother-in-law, Rüdiger Schleicher, were murdered at the Lehrterstrasse 3 prison. Eberhard Bethge was also held in Lehrtestrasse 3, but was released on April 25 as the Russian army approached.

H. Fischer-Hüllstrung, a camp doctor at Flossenbürg, wrote about the day of Bonhoeffer's execution:

> On the morning of that day between five and six o'clock the prisoners, among them Admiral Canaris, General Oster, General Thomas, and *Reichgerichtsrat* Sack were taken from their cells, and the verdicts of the court martial read out to them. Through the half-open door in one room of the huts I saw Pastor Bonhoeffer, before taking off his prison garb, kneeling on the floor praying fervently to his God. I was most deeply moved by the way this lovable man prayed, so devout and so certain that God heard his prayer. At the place of execution, he again said a short prayer and then climbed the steps to the gallows, brave and composed. His death ensued after a few seconds. In the almost fifty years I worked as a doctor, I have hardly ever seen a man die so entirely submissive to the will of God.[4]

The news of Dietrich Bonhoeffer's death was first known by Visser't Hooft in Geneva, and word was later sent to England, where Bishop Bell informed the Leibholz family in Oxford. On July 27, Bishop Bell conducted a memorial service in Kingsway, London, which recognized Bonhoeffer's great contribution to the ecumenical movement. It was while listening to the broadcast of this service that Bonhoeffer's parents learned that their son was dead. Maria finally learned of her fiancée's death after unsuccessfully tracing his footsteps all over southern Germany. Later, Maria informed her family that "Dietrich is dead."

CHAPTER ONE

Jesus Christ Is the Center, Yet Hidden

"Christ the Center" was the title chosen for the 1966 English translation of Bonhoeffer's lectures on Christology. This title summarizes the essence of his personal life as well as his theological orientation. While the challenges of his life at times led him away from the organization and orthodoxy of Christian tradition, there can be little doubt that Jesus Christ was, for Dietrich Bonhoeffer, the center of all reality.

Three Bonhoeffer scholars have addressed this centrality: "Christology was at all stages of his pilgrimage the inward law of his thinking, the definitive thought . . . the whole significance of his work."[5] "Christology [was] the guiding principle . . . the foundation and heart of his theology."[6] "Bonhoeffer's central theme—Christ present—thus stands for the presence of God in reality and the presence of reality to God."[7]

Bonhoeffer's best friend and biographer, Eberhard Bethge, considered the summer of 1933 to be "the high point of Bonhoeffer's academic career, for now he lectured on Christology."[8] A decade later, writing from Tegel Prison on April 30, 1944, Bonhoeffer asked Bethge, "Who is Christ actually for us today?" What first might appear a simple question, begging a simple answer, is really a profound question born of serious theological reflection. This radical question did not suddenly surface as a result of his prison interrogation or the despair caused by months of incarceration. Rather, it is further evidence that Dietrich Bonhoeffer maintained a living, dynamic relationship with Jesus Christ throughout his life as pastor, professor, and prisoner.

There are countless references to the centrality of Jesus Christ in Bonhoeffer's writings. He prayed and thought and acted in constant awareness of Christ's presence, and nearly everything he wrote shows traces of that awareness.

It is quite amazing that at the age of twenty-seven Bonhoeffer had such a comprehensive grasp of Christology and its importance for the church. This aptitude is evident in the lectures he gave at the university on Wednesdays and Saturdays between May 3 and July 22, 1933.[9] Although the young lecturer could barely be distinguished in appearance from many of his students, it quickly became apparent that his teaching had great authority and deep authenticity.

Bonhoeffer's introduction to his lectures published as *Christology* presents the subject in a profound and creative way. In it he insists that any speaking about Jesus Christ must begin in silence: "The silence of the church is silence before the Word. In proclaiming Christ, the church falls on its knees in silence before the inexpressible . . . that is obedient affirmation of God's revelation, which takes place through the Word."[10] Bonhoeffer learned to respect God's Word in this way from the man who was his single greatest theological mentor, Karl Barth. Bonhoeffer repeated Barth's radical view that any knowledge of God begins with Jesus Christ.

Bonhoeffer suggested that most discussion about Jesus Christ has focused on *how* the divine became human, that is, *how* the Word became flesh. However, Bonhoeffer asserts that, since God has spoken to the world in the person of Jesus Christ, "the question of *who* is the [real] question about transcendence."[11] While the question of *how* is immanent (asked from within this world), the question of *who* is transcendent (asked about matters from outside this world).

Bonhoeffer also disagreed with many common conceptions about Christ's presence in the world. "Jesus is the Christ who is present now . . . in time and space."[12] Bonhoeffer disagrees with those who think of Christ's presence as ". . . the influence that emanates from him . . . Christ as power but not as person."[13] Jesus Christ is not just a historical figure to be studied in hindsight, but a living presence.

Throughout history, philosophers and theologians have expended significant energy contemplating God's essence. Bonhoeffer thinks that all such human speculation about God's essence is fruitless because the only real source of knowledge about God is Jesus Christ: "I can never think of Jesus Christ in his being-in-itself, but only in his relatedness to me."[14] John A. Phillips writes: "The heart of Bonhoeffer's [Christology] lectures is his argument that the . . . personal structure of Christ is *pro-me*."[15]

Having decided that all discussion about Jesus Christ 1) begins in silence and openness before God's Word, 2) asks the proper question about *who* we are dealing with, not about *how* God can become a person, 3) understands that Jesus Christ is a present person, not simply a historical figure, and 4) cannot expect to know God in Godself, only the God who is present "for me," Bonhoeffer then describes the form and place of Jesus Christ. Phillips notes, "Two questions are thus proper to Christology: In what *form* is Christ present *pro me*, and *where* is Christ present *pro me*?[16]

Jesus Christ is the Center and Present in the Preached Word

Far from an invisible spiritual presence that people seek to tap into through prayer and meditation, Jesus Christ takes on the form of audible words spoken in an ordinary sermon.

> Christ . . . is the Word in the form of the living Word to humankind . . . [not] in the form of an idea . . . the Word in the form of address is only possible as word between two persons. . . .Thus Christ is not timelessly and universally accessible as an idea. . . . This Christ who is the Word in person is present in the word of the church. His presence is, by nature,

his existence as preaching. . . . The sermon is the form of the present Christ. . . .[17]

It does not matter whether the preacher is eloquent or boring, long-winded or brief, profound or trite, each parishioner is challenged to experience Jesus Christ in the human words of ordinary preaching. Bonhoeffer thought the church could be a stumbling block for some, because one could easily miss Christ's Word by refusing to listen to an ordinary sermon. The proclaimed Word is the first form Jesus Christ takes.

Jesus Christ Is the Center and Present in the Sacraments of Baptism and Communion

According to Bonhoeffer,

> Sacrament exists only where God . . . names an element, speaks to it, and hallows it with the particular word God has for it by giving it its name. . . . Not everything in nature or everything in bodily form is destined to become sacrament. Christ's presence is . . . preaching and sacrament.[18]

> The Word in the sacrament is the Word in bodily form. . . . the sacrament does not represent the "Word," for only that which is not present can be represented. . . . The sacrament, in the form of nature, engages human beings in their nature.[19]

Bonhoeffer was heavily influenced by Luther, and he reminded us that, "Luther says . . . [God] is everywhere. But you will not catch him unless he offers himself to you. . . . Christ is even in the rustling leaves . . . but his presence is not obvious; he is not there for you, not *pro me*."[20] In the sacraments of Baptism and Holy Communion, Jesus Christ is present, in, with, and under the water, bread, and wine. Just as God chooses to speak God's word through an ordinary sermon, so does God choose to be physically present in the tangible elements of the sacraments. The sacraments are the second form Jesus Christ takes.

Jesus Christ Is the Center and Present in the Church-Community

A third form Jesus Christ takes is the church-community. Since Pentecost, the church is Christ's body, imperfect and broken, yet filled with God's spirit (1 Corinthians 12:12-30).

> The Church-Community is the form he takes. . . . It is not a mere image; the Church-Community is the body of Christ. It is so in reality. . . . Christ being in the Church-Community is like his being as Word, a being in the form of the stumbling block.[21]

Consistent with Bonhoeffer's belief that Jesus Christ is living and present, the church-community does not merely represent the body of Christ, it *is* the body of Christ. Just as the imperfect words of the preacher provide Christ's living Word, and the ordinary elements of water, bread, and wine provide Christ's promise and nourishment, so the motley bodies of brothers and sisters in the church provide Christ's physical presence. Jesus Christ is the center, concretely present in the forms of Word, sacraments, and church-community. Now we proceed to the "places" where we meet Jesus Christ.

Jesus Christ Is the Hidden Center of Humankind, History, and Nature

"It is the nature of Christ's person to be in the center . . . the mediator . . . for humankind . . . for history . . . for nature."[22] Bonhoeffer believed that Jesus' centrality in a person's life is not known externally. One's personality does not automatically reveal, nor do one's actions necessarily display, that Jesus Christ is the center of one's life. Affirming Jesus Christ as the center of humanity empowers one to live out the blessings of that life-giving presence. There is no need to invoke God's presence because Jesus Christ is already there. Christian faith affirms what natural sight cannot observe.

> The center of our existence is [not] the center of our personality. This is not a psychological statement, but rather an ontological/theological one, because it refers not to our personality, but rather to the persons we are before God. . . . Christ is not the center that we can see is here but rather the center according to our faith.[23]

Through faith, Bonhoeffer says, we can simply trust God's presence. God's presence is the center of our lives, regardless of feelings or appearance.

"The church should be understood as the center of history . . . between promise and fulfillment . . . the hidden center of the state."[24] Jesus Christ is certainly present in the church, but Bonhoeffer goes beyond that when he affirms Jesus as the center of all history. Just as the presence of Jesus Christ in the Word, sacraments, church-community, and humankind is hidden, so Jesus Christ is the hidden center of history. God promises that God's purpose will be realized with the unfolding of history. Human history is under God's providence, and recognizing Christ's centrality has an enormous influence on how we order our lives. Much like the hidden presence of Christ in humanity, Jesus' centrality in history is not visibly known. Many wonder where God is when disaster strikes. Yet, even among brokenness and corruption, faith can affirm what sight cannot see—glimpses of hope and signs of healing pointing toward a future of God's perfect *shalom*.

Although Bonhoeffer does not go into detail about Jesus Christ being the center of nature, it would seem that he affirms the hidden presence of Jesus Christ in every dimension of reality, including humankind, history, and nature: "Christ cannot be proved to be the redeeming creation within nature; he can only be preached as such."[25]

Perhaps concerns about the environment are just another expression of humankind's desire to affirm Jesus Christ as the center of nature. From the Bible we learn of God's original design for the universe, its subsequent fall from perfection, and God's vision for its fulfillment. Jesus Christ, the Word made flesh, is at the center of nature's final redemption.

The Hiddenness of Jesus Christ

It is important to add that Jesus' presence is hidden not only at the center of humankind, history, and nature, but also in the Word, sacraments and church community. God is revealed in ways that contradict the expected. Christ's presence in the Word must be experienced through ordinary sermons, in the sacraments through ordinary elements of water, bread, and wine, and in the church-community through ordinary, even broken, persons. God calls upon the church to listen for God's Word and experience God's presence "ever anew"[26] and ever "in silence."[27]

The discipline needed to protect God's hidden presence in the world was something Bonhoeffer spoke about in his lectures at Finkenwalde, alluded to in the "costly grace" section of *Discipleship*, and specifically referred to in *Letters and Papers from Prison*. In his letter of May 5, 1944, Bonhoeffer wrote, "That means an 'arcane discipline' must be reestablished, through which the mysteries of the Christian faith are sheltered against profanation."[28]

Bonhoeffer is referring to an ancient church practice, focused in baptism, in which prospective church members were required to display their knowledge about the Christian faith, after having gone through a three-year period of instruction and mentoring, before they were allowed to join the church. This early church practice, called *disciplina arcani*, was a way for the church to both carefully guard and graciously share Jesus Christ with the world. The term *disciplina arcani* can be most accurately translated as "responsible sharing of the mystery of

Christian faith."[29] Some have thought that the term implied that the discipline was to be secret, rather than that the secret needed to be disciplined. Many have limited this important concept to refer only to the need for private, inner-church activities like prayer, sacraments, and worship, when it should actually refer to all the ways the mystery of Christian faith is responsibly shared with the world, including the public and political.

That Jesus Christ is the center, yet hidden, is an insight of Bonhoeffer's that is both challenging and helpful. Faith describes a belief that is not dependant on visible proof. Bonhoeffer assures us that "in, with, and under" the ordinary words of a sermon, the water of baptism, the bread and wine of communion, the lives of people, the events of history, and the substance of nature, God is present and Jesus Christ is central. The church is called to responsibly protect and proclaim that hidden, yet central, presence. After the *Christology* lectures lay the foundation for affirming Jesus Christ as the center, Bonhoeffer's thought continued to reflect the centrality of Jesus Christ, even while confined in a Gestapo prison.

In the same year that Bonhoeffer was lecturing at the University of Berlin about Jesus Christ as the center of history, the Nazis were proclaiming and enforcing another center: Adolf Hitler. In 1933 Bonhoeffer spoke on the radio challenging the dangerous view that was engulfing Germany, a view that placed one human being—the *Führer*—at the center of humankind and history. Bonhoeffer's Christ-centered understanding of reality played a large role in his ability to critique this evil hijacking of history.

In the spring of 1934, this same Christ-centered understanding of history would find its way into the opening paragraph of the Barmen Declaration: "Jesus Christ, as he is attested to us in Holy Scripture, is the one Word of God whom we have to hear, and whom we have to trust and obey in life and in death" ("The Barmen Declaration," May 1934).[30]

Karl Barth was the principle author of the Declaration, and Bonhoeffer basically agreed with its Christ-centered focus. When in 1935 Bonhoeffer was called back from parish ministry in England to direct one of the five seminaries that would train pastors to serve Confessing Church congregations (which opposed the Nazified Reich Church under Bishop Ludwig Müller), he would shape the worship, teaching, service, and fellowship of the seminary community around the centrality of the living presence of Jesus Christ. He wrote *Life Together* to describe this Christ-centered community, a book that continues to inspire Christian disciples today. He also wrote *Discipleship* around this same time, attempting to help Christian people bond their lives more closely to Jesus Christ.

When Bonhoeffer wrote *Discipleship*, he was still quite focused on Jesus Christ as the center of the *church*. By 1941, as his reflections and writings on ethics were progressing and he became actively engaged in conspiratorial activity, the scope of his understanding of Christ's centrality became broader than the church. As he began to believe that the work of God lay in defeating Hitler's evil regime, he came to see that Jesus Christ, albeit in hidden form, was at the center of the circle of those conspiring to assassinate the *Führer*. Through his brother-in-law, Hans von Dohnanyi, Bonhoeffer came to believe that only Hitler's death would end the genocide of Jews and other undesirables. It was Bonhoeffer's belief in the hidden centrality of Jesus Christ in the work of the military resistance that led him to distance himself from some friends, even those in the Confessing Church, and risk association with the conspirators.

During Bonhoeffer's imprisonment at Tegel Prison, he wrote letters to family and friends, some poetry, a drama, and a novel. In these now classic writings, we see an extremely intelligent, highly gifted, deeply sensitive, Christ-centered human being. Although Bonhoeffer's thought changed in light of new experiences, it was never for him a question *if* Jesus Christ was present and central, but rather *what* that presence was calling him to do.

The Bible Bonhoeffer used[31] was returned to him by the prison guards on April 14. He used it daily for devotional reading and study. He included some biblical references in most of his letters written to family and friends as he tried to see his life in light of God's presence and purpose. He often framed his thoughts by using current church festivals and commemorations. Only three weeks after his arrest and imprisonment he wrote to his parents,

> I would really like you to know that I am celebrating a happy Easter here. What is so liberating about Good Friday and Easter is the fact that our thoughts are pulled far beyond our personal circumstances to the ultimate meaning of all life, suffering, and indeed everything that happens, and this gives us great hope.[32]

On August 24, he mentioned in another letter to his parents how a certain Scripture passage gave him strength. "Then early this morning the *Moravian Daily Text* moved me strangely: 'And I will grant peace in the land, and you shall lie down, and no one shall make you afraid.'"[33] He increasingly dwelt on passages from the Old Testament, as in his December 5, 1943, letter to Bethge:

> By the way, I notice more and more how much I am thinking and perceiving things in line with the Old Testament; thus in recent months I have been reading much more the Old than the New Testament. Only when one knows that the name of God may not be uttered may one sometimes speak the name of Jesus Christ.[34]

Bonhoeffer's serious and sustained theological dialogue with Bethge began on April 30, 1944. He speaks about the centrality of Jesus Christ in his letters to Bethge on April 30, May 29, and June 27:

I'd like to speak of God not at the boundaries but in the center. . . . God is the beyond in the midst of our lives. . . . God is the center of life and doesn't just "turn up" when we have unsolved problems to be solved. . . . But Christ takes hold of human beings in the midst of their lives.[35]

Bethge has said that, of all the letters he received from Bonhoeffer in prison, the words of July 21, the day following the unsuccessful attempt to assassinate Hitler, were the most meaningful to him.

In the last few years I have come to know and understand more and more the profound this-worldliness of Christianity. . . . I am still discovering to this day, that one only learns to have faith by living in the full this-worldliness of life . . . then one throws oneself completely into the arms of God, and this is what I call this-worldliness: living fully in the midst of life's tasks, questions, successes and failures, experiences, and perplexities—then one takes seriously no longer one's own sufferings but rather the suffering of God in the world. . . . And I think this is faith. . . .[36]

No more telling words could be written about the centrality of Christ for Bonhoeffer than those which close this July 21 letter to Bethge. With the failure of the July 20th plot, Bonhoeffer's hope for a quick end to the Nazi nightmare, as well as an end to his imprisonment, was effectively gone. He wrote: "May God lead us kindly through these times, but above all, may God lead us to himself."[37] Only moments before his execution on April 9, 1945, Dietrich Bonhoeffer said to Payne Best: "This is the end, for me the beginning of life."[38] From his formal lectures on *Christology* in 1933, through every chapter of his pastoral, professorial, and conspiratorial life, and finally to his death, the central, yet hidden, reality of life for Bonhoeffer was Jesus Christ.

CHAPTER TWO

Life with Jesus Christ Is Communal, Yet Personal

In chapter one, we saw that Bonhoeffer's theology is dependent on affirming Jesus Christ as the center of all things. We now turn from the centrality of Jesus Christ to living with Jesus Christ in community with others.

The culmination of Bonhoeffer's doctoral studies was the oral defense of his dissertation *Sanctorum Communio*) on December 17, 1927, at the University of Berlin, after which he was awarded the Licentiate in Theology degree *summa cum laude*. Karl Barth later praised Bonhoeffer's dissertation, saying, "I openly confess that I have misgivings whether I can even maintain the high level reached by Bonhoeffer, saying no less in my own words and context . . . than did this young man so many years ago."[39]

Bonhoeffer states in the dissertation that sociality is not only of the essence of human community, but also constitutive of human personality and intrinsic to Christian spirituality:

> Human beings, as spirit, are necessarily created in a community—that human spirit in general is woven into the web of sociality. . . . God does not desire a history of individual human beings, but the history of the human community.[40]

Bonhoeffer continues: "Only in interaction with one another is the spirit of human beings ever revealed; this is the essence of spirit, to be oneself through being in the other."[41]

Clifford Green succinctly characterizes the substance of Bonhoeffer's dissertation (and theology), saying, "Bonhoeffer's

Christology is simultaneously incarnational and communal."[42] Green follows Bonhoeffer's discussion of the social dimension of humanity and Christianity beginning with Bonhoeffer's dissertation, continuing through the social ontology of *Act and Being*, the social liberation of individuals in *Discipleship*, the social responsibility involved in *Ethics*, and finally the social solidarity required of all people as explored in the *Letters and Papers from Prison*.[43]

Bonhoeffer argued in his doctoral dissertation, and then integrated into virtually every chapter of his life, that individuals can only know themselves while in community. It is impossible for individuals to know themselves, even love themselves, all by themselves. One's very self is a creation, a product of relationships and community. For Bonhoeffer, sociality/community is not an optional activity; sociality is what, in essence, defines who people are.

Within Bonhoeffer's doctoral dissertation lies his hard work on "Social Philosophy and Sociology," "Social Basic-Relation," and "Christian Concepts of Persons." His work was creative and thought provoking to the point that his cousin, Hans-Christoph von Hase, remarked in a letter of October 13, 1930: "There will not be many who really understand [his argument]; the Barthians won't because of the sociology, and the sociologists because of Barth."[44]

Bonhoeffer concludes chapter one of *Sanctorum Communio* by saying: "The Christian concept of the person is really exhibited only in sociality . . . human spirit generally is possible and real only in sociality . . . only then can we give a fundamental refutation of individualistic social atomism."[45] Over and against the individualism found in most every discipline since the Enlightenment, Bonhoeffer proposed a view of persons and church that was communal, not private. Further, he grounded this view in the revelation of God in Jesus Christ. Beginning with God's Word, Christians are essentially shaped in community. This corporate view of Christian life has significant implications for preaching and evangelism.

A significant amount of Christian preaching has revolved around the invitation to individuals for a personal relationship with Jesus Christ. While well intentioned, this call to faith often implies an individual transaction with God that may or may not need to involve other people. Often repentance and forgiveness are encouraged to make individuals right with God. While such preaching qualifies as what Bonhoeffer would later call "religious" (see chapter five), it is not Christian if it excludes the Christ who is essentially known in community. Other people do not exist as optional blessings for a life of faith; other people are essential components of a true relationship with the living God.

The community of family, friends, and church gathered around the baptismal font is not a social nicety, but a sacramental necessity. Gathering communally around the sacramental table with bread and wine is not a group activity because others happen to be available. Holy Communion is an expression of the incarnation of Jesus Christ, and, therefore, the presence of others is essential for a true experience of the living God. If and when, in emergency situations, the sacraments are administered to individuals by one member of the community, that one member is acting on behalf of the community, still expressing the sociality of the event. Does Christian faith imply a personal relationship with Jesus Christ? Absolutely! Is that relationship private? No! Life with Jesus Christ is essentially communal.

Spirituality, as opposed to organized religion, is an increasingly popular, though certainly not new, trend. Studies have revealed a desire among many people for a more individualistic faith, often as a reaction to negative experiences in church communities. Bonhoeffer's conviction that life in Jesus Christ is communal, yet personal, opposes this. He would likely say that persons desiring such a personal spiritual experience may be seeking God, but they will not experience God "in Christ," unless they take part in the community.

Bonhoeffer believed that community is what constitutes the blessing, beauty, and brokenness of Christian faith. Preaching and evangelism are invitations for individuals to become involved in the church, the body of Christ on earth. To be related to God is to be related to people. According to Bonhoeffer, life with Jesus Christ is always communal.

In *The Communion of Saints*, Bonhoeffer laid out the theoretical foundation for life in Jesus Christ. Five years later, in his lectures on "The Nature of the Church," Bonhoeffer "developed along more practical lines the finely tuned analysis of *Sanctorum Communio*."[46] At this same time, Bonhoeffer often gathered student groups together for the express purpose of living out the communal nature of Jesus Christ. Evening discussions, along with weekend excursions in the country, helped them to experience the concrete reality of the church corporate, the communion of saints.

Before returning from England in the spring of 1935, Bonhoeffer observed the ordered life of the Society of the Sacred Mission in Kelham and the Community of the Resurrection in Mirfield. These, along with some visits to a Methodist college and a Quaker center, helped him envision concrete Christian community.

Without question the most significant context for Bonhoeffer's practical application of communal life in Jesus Christ was his experience shared with ordinands preparing for ministry in the Confessing Church between 1935 and 1937. "The community experience of Finkenwalde was memorable because it provided a unique occasion to test out in concrete experience his understanding of what a church could and should be."[47]

As the director of Finkenwalde, one of five seminaries established out of the Dahlem Synod of the Confessing Church in 1934, Bonhoeffer had the responsibility and flexibility to structure a program that would adequately prepare the ordinands for parish ministry in challenging settings. Confessing Church congregations were not officially endorsed by the Reich Church, so great courage and deep conviction were required of pastors serving in these places. Bonhoeffer knew that not only academic preparation, but also spiritual readiness were needed to sustain these pastors. For two and one-half years he oversaw five groups (149 candidates) of those who, having completed university studies in theology, now needed practical training and personal discipline before ordination and parish assignment.

When the Finkenwalde seminary was closed by the Gestapo in the fall of 1937, Bonhoeffer felt an increasing need to record the communal experiences of those years. After helping his twin sister and her family emigrate to England in the fall of 1938, Bonhoeffer spent a brief yet concentrated time with Bethge in Göttingen. After only four weeks there, he had written *Life Together*. Geffrey B. Kelly writes: "*Life Together* was hardly a study in abstraction. The reality behind the book was the church in its most palpable, somatic form, the Christian community."[48]

What then was "life together" at Finkenwalde like? For sure, it was both Christ-centered and communal. The chapter divisions of *Life Together* correspond to the categories that Bonhoeffer thought were most important: community, the day together, the day alone, service, confession, and the Lord's Supper. Each of these elements reinforced his fundamental conviction (already set forth in *The Communion of Saints*) of "Christ existing as community."[49]

In the Finkenwalde seminary community, each day began in silence until God's Word was first spoken during the opening worship. What a profound way to model the priority of God's Word for each day of life together! Morning worship included readings from the Old Testament, the New Testament, the Psalms, hymn singing, extemporaneous prayer, and—once a week—commentary on the Scripture texts by Bonhoeffer. After breakfast each morning there was a thirty-minute period of private meditation for all the seminarians, which was to be focused on a single text used for the whole week. The remainder of each morning was spent in lectures and discussions around theological topics. It was during this time of morning study that Bonhoeffer presented the lectures that would later become *Discipleship*. Each morning concluded with another time of hymn singing. Afternoons varied, but could include recreation, relaxation, reading, and community service. The day ended as it began, with worship and hearing God's Word. Holy Communion was celebrated once each month and was considered the high point in the community's life. Personal confession was encouraged by Bonhoeffer as proper preparation for receiving the sacrament.

In the afterword of *Life Together*, Gerhard Müller and Albrecht Schönherr nicely summarize the three essential requirements of life together:

> First, Christians need brothers and sisters because they represent and authenticate the origin of salvation outside of myself, as those who are given to me and yet are not under my control. Christians need their brothers and sisters as the objective bearers and proclaimers of the divine Word of forgiveness and grace. . . . Second, just as salvation comes from Jesus Christ alone—and the community of brothers and sisters is to be understood as an expression of God's nearness that has become flesh, as the mode of God's appearance— so the broken original—community with God and human beings is restored only through Christ. . . . Third, the nature of the church as community is encountered in the Bible under the metaphor of the "body of Christ." . . . In their familial togetherness they are a hopeful sign of the unity between the freedom and love that constitutes the essence of God.[50]

Regarding community (chapter one of *Life Together*), Bonhoeffer writes:

The Christian cannot simply take for granted the privilege of living among other Christians. . . . The physical presence of other Christians is a source of incomparable joy and strength to the believer.[51]

Bonhoeffer would later realize how precious that physical presence really was when he experienced solitary confinement in Tegel Prison:

The prisoner, the sick person, the Christian living in the diaspora recognizes in the nearness of a fellow Christian a physical sign of the gracious presence of the triune God. . . . Christian community means community through Jesus Christ and in Jesus Christ.[52]

Bonhoeffer defines "through and in" Jesus Christ by contrasting the imperfect, human community gathered around Jesus Christ with the "wishful image" and "wishful dreaming" of people's ideal religious community: "Christian community is not an ideal we have to realize, but rather a reality created by God in Christ in which we may participate."[53] *Life Together* addresses individual faith and community self-image: "Just as Christians should not be constantly feeling the pulse of their spiritual life, so too the Christian community has not been given to us by God for us to be continually taking its temperature. . . . Christian community is a gift of God to which we have no claim."[54] He also contrasts emotional love, which is self-centered, and spiritual love, which is other-centered. His argument puts spiritual love at the center of Christian life together, criticizing emotional love for its destructive, selfish nature.

In chapter two, Bonhoeffer details the proper use of the Psalms as the "vicarious prayer of Christ" for the church.[55] Reading the Scriptures, singing together, praying, eating meals together, daily work, and worship as a community at the end of each day critiques any spirituality that is merely private. To repeat, life with Jesus Christ is communal, yet personal.

However, chapter three follows with a clear warning to all who would promote only togetherness. "Whoever cannot be alone should beware of community. Whoever cannot stand being in community should beware of being alone."[56] The day alone includes meditation, prayer, and intercession. If used properly, the time one spends alone strengthens the community just as the time spent in community gives one support for being alone. Aloneness, which has its place in the day, is not the same as the privatization of Christian faith.

Chapter four on service speaks about the ministry Christians have with and for one another. Caring for each other involves learning when to speak and when to remain silent:

> [L]istening can be a greater service than speaking. . . . Christians are [often] talking even when they should be listening. "Active helpfulness," like "bearing with others," is crucial to authentic service in Christian community. Proclaiming God's Word, often in admonition, is also a necessity for a healthy, Christ-centered community.[57]

Chapter five, "Confession and the Lord's Supper," includes some of the most beautiful and helpful material yet offered. The high point of Bonhoeffer's practical writings on life in Jesus Christ could well be the following words that open chapter five:

> It is possible that Christians may remain lonely in spite of daily worship together, prayer together, and all their community through service—that the final breakthrough to community does not occur precisely because they enjoy community with one another as pious believers, but not with one another as those lacking piety, as sinners. For the pious community permits no one to be a sinner. Hence all have to conceal their sins from themselves and from the community. We are not allowed to be sinners. Many

Christians would be unimaginably horrified if a real sinner were suddenly to turn up among the pious. So we remain alone with our sin, trapped in lies and hypocrisy, for we are in fact sinners. However, the grace of the gospel, which is so hard for the pious to comprehend, confronts us with the truth. It says to us, you are a sinner, a great, unholy sinner. Now come, as the sinner that you are, to your God who loves you. . . . The mask you wear in the presence of other people won't get you anywhere in the presence of God. God wants to see you as you are, wants to be gracious to you. . . . You are allowed to be a sinner. Thank God for that; God loves the sinner but hates the sin.[58]

Although chapter five is entitled "Confession and the Lord's Supper," virtually all of the content relates to confession, which "serves the Christian community especially as a preparation for participation in the Lord's Supper."[59] Bonhoeffer divides this chapter into the various "break throughs" which occur as a result of the confession of sins. He encourages honest conversation between people where "they experience the presence of God in the reality of the other. . . . In the one other Christian to whom I confess my sins and by whom my sins are declared forgiven, I meet the whole congregation."[60] The breakthroughs in concrete confession are community, the cross, new life, and assurance.

First, Bonhoeffer expresses a common hindrance to community: "Sin wants to remain unknown. . . . In the darkness of what is left unsaid sin poisons the whole being of a person [which] can happen in the midst of a pious community."[61] When sins are confessed they are exposed to the light of day and to God, and in doing so they lose their power. At this point the community, not the individual, bears the sin and gives it to God. People can then "find community for the first time . . . [and be] allowed to be a sinner and still enjoy the grace of God."[62] This is where Bonhoeffer's Lutheran heritage, specifically a believer's status as *simil justis et peccator* (simultaneously justified and sinful), shines through with particular brilliance. Through confession, individual brokenness is swallowed up into the corporate body and is reconciled. This is what leads to true human community.

Second, a breakthrough to the cross comes from honest confession. In short, confession removes pride, and that experience opens the door for a deeper understanding of the humiliation of Jesus Christ—the cross. "In the profound spiritual and physical pain of humiliation . . . we experience the cross of Jesus."[63]

Third, honest confession occasions a breakthrough to new life. "Confession is a conversion."[64] Bonhoeffer claims that the old life has passed away when sin is hated, confessed, and forgiven. What was promised in baptism is made new with each confession and absolution. With the death and destruction of sin's heavy weight, new life is experienced.

Finally, assurance is a breakthrough for Christians practicing confession and receiving forgiveness. In contrast with a more generic acknowledgment of all our sins before God (which Bonhoeffer thought was the equivalent of forgiving oneself), "the other believer breaks the circle of self-deception. . . . [We] experience the presence of God in the reality of the other. . . . God gives us this assurance through one another."[65]

Bonhoeffer suggests: "Only another Christian who is under the cross can hear my confession. . . . Whoever has once been appalled by the horror of their own sin, which nailed Jesus to the cross, will no longer be appalled by even the most serious sin of another Christian. . . . In the presence of a psychologist I can only be sick; in the presence of another Christian I can be a sinner."[66] It is in the shadow of such honest confession and renewed community that the Lord's

Supper is experienced. It becomes a "joyous occasion. . . . The life together of Christians under the Word has reached its fulfillment in the sacrament."[67]

What began with Bonhoeffer's academic doctoral work, where Bonhoeffer first addressed the communal nature of life in Jesus Christ, found practical and personal expression in Finkenwalde and was documented in *Life Together*.

CHAPTER THREE

Discipleship Is Bonding with Jesus Christ, Yet Breaking with the World

Perhaps Bonhoeffer's most well known book is *Discipleship*.[68] It was the most widely read of his books while he was alive and the first book of his to be printed in English in 1948. *Discipleship* is based on Bonhoeffer's lectures at Finkenwalde, and it includes a significant section on the Sermon on the Mount. With roots preceding the rise of National Socialism in 1933, *Discipleship* should be viewed against the backdrop of Hitler's Germany. Although the context has changed, *Discipleship* continues to be extremely relevant for life in the church today.

No one derives ideas *ex nihilo* (out of nothing), and Bonhoeffer is no exception. His thoughts on discipleship and his lectures on the same topic in the mid-1930s are the result of personal experience, biblical study, hermeneutics (interpretation), and historical awareness.

Dietrich Bonhoeffer considered church life in twentieth-century Germany to be somewhat lifeless and perhaps even useless. He did not fail to notice the cautious reserve of his father nor the cynicism of his brothers towards the church. Active church membership for many at that time had far more to do with social custom and cultural nicety than with following Jesus Christ. But something deep within Bonhoeffer made him desire a church that would make a difference:

> When he was about fourteen, for instance, they tried to convince him that he was taking the path of least

resistance, and that the church to which he proposed to devote himself was a poor, feeble, boring, petty, and bourgeois institution, but he confidently replied, "In that case I shall reform it."[69]

Part of Bonhoeffer's motivation for reviving authentic Christian discipleship came from his desire to make a unique and significant contribution. In a family often critical of the church, he set out to "reform it."

Second, Bonhoeffer took the Bible very seriously. His intellectual gifts allowed him to go far beyond the basics, stretching the boundaries of accepted dogma. Bonhoeffer addressed questions that others deemed either unimportant or threatening. Like Luther, Augustine, and other pillars of Christian tradition, Dietrich Bonhoeffer expected to find the living God through biblical study.

Third, he faithfully, yet creatively, attempted to interpret God's Word for his time and place. At the center of Bonhoeffer's *Discipleship* is the Sermon on the Mount, specifically an explication on the Beatitudes. Interpreting the Bible correctly was of paramount importance for Bonhoeffer.

Fourth, any encounter with Bonhoeffer's thoughts on discipleship will need to factor in his historical awareness. The threat of Nazi ideology to humanity, plus the temptation for the state church to conform to that ideology, was an enormous challenge, especially for Christians. Bonhoeffer quickly realized that a lifeless church would not have the strength required to confront such a threat. Following Jesus in spite of this threat would require extraordinary courage and sacrifice.

Cheap Grace Versus Costly Grace

"Cheap grace is the mortal enemy of our church. Our struggle today is for costly grace."[70] It is with these explosive words that Bonhoeffer launches his exposition on *Discipleship*. Although in subsequent chapters he develops details for following Jesus Christ, a central element of *Discipleship* is the dialectical tension of grace and obedience inherent in Christian life, what he refers to as "costly grace." Ever the Lutheran, Bonhoeffer held high the Reformation banners of *sola gratia* (grace alone) and *sola fide* (faith alone). The gift of God's grace in Jesus Christ was the beginning and the end, the foundation and capstone of divine interaction with the world. He well knew the clear distinction drawn by the sixteenth-century reformers between gospel and law, grace and obedience, faith and actions. God's grace through Jesus Christ (grace to be received through faith) was never to be confused with humanity's actions for God (obedience expressed through actions). However, he thought obedience to that grace was lacking in his time; the inauthenticity of the church's actions cheapened its gracious message.

Bonhoeffer defines "cheap grace" as "grace as doctrine, as principle, as system . . . justification of sin but not the sinner . . . preaching forgiveness without repentance . . . grace without discipleship . . . without the cross."[71] He saw cheap grace as the result of detaching the work of God in Jesus Christ (gospel and grace) from the response and obedience required of those who receive it (law and obedience). Once detached, law and obedience could be diminished so that gospel and grace would be amplified. Bonhoeffer contrasts "cheap grace" with "costly grace," which "must be sought again and again, the gift which has to be asked for, the door at which one has to knock . . . costly, because it condemns sin . . . costly to God, because it costs God the life of God's son."[72]

It is against the backdrop of Lutheran theology, which often hyper-focuses on the grace of God, simultaneously diminishing the concomitant need for obedience, that Bonhoeffer draws this helpful contrast of cheap and costly grace: "Like ravens we have gathered around the carcass of cheap grace. From it we have imbibed the poison which has killed the following of Jesus among us."[73] He speaks further of the danger of separating grace and obedience:

But if grace is a principled presupposition of my Christian life, then in advance I have justification of whatever sins I commit. . . . I can now sin on the basis of this grace; the world is in principle justified by grace. . . . Everything remains as before. . . . I am liberated from following Jesus—by cheap grace, which has to be the bitterest enemy of discipleship. . . . Grace as presupposition is grace at its cheapest; grace as conclusion is costly grace.[74]

Bonhoeffer is recasting an experience of the early church as recorded in the book of James. Already in the first century, the followers of Jesus were wrestling with the tension of grace and obedience inherent in Christian life. The second chapter of James addresses the relationship of faith and action: "In the same way, faith by itself, if it is not accompanied by action is dead" (James 2:17). Also, in the same chapter: "You see that a person is justified by what he does and not by faith alone" (James 2:24).

Martin Luther was reacting to an exaggerated emphasis in the late-medieval church on works required for salvation when he suggested that the book of James be removed from the New Testament because such works could obscure God's grace. In *Discipleship* Dietrich Bonhoeffer not only shows the importance of maintaining a close relationship between grace and obedience, but insists upon it. "Only those who in following Christ leave everything they have can stand and say that they are justified solely by grace."[75] It is important to note that, according to Bonhoeffer, it was primarily Luther's followers who drove the wedge separating faith and works; Luther knew well the tension—and necessity—of both grace and obedience. "Justification is a gift of grace, but it is not a gift that renders Christians free from responsibility."[76]

Another influential figure for Bonhoeffer was Søren Kierkegaard, the Danish Lutheran philosopher/theologian of the late nineteenth century. Kierkegaard, like Bonhoeffer, observed a church whose word and witness had grown impotent due to a similar detaching of obedience from grace. Since membership in both the Danish state church and the German state church came through baptism for virtually all citizens regardless of response, grace was distributed without any commitment. Kierkegaard, like Bonhoeffer, understood Jesus' ultimate, costly demand on a person's life. Bonhoeffer writes: "We therefore simply have to try to understand grace and discipleship again in correct relationship to each other."[77]

The Call to Discipleship—Obedience and Suffering

Following his explosive introduction on the contrast between cheap and costly grace, Bonhoeffer discusses the dynamics of bonding with Jesus Christ.

The call to discipleship begins with the simple words of Jesus, found in Mark 2:14: "Follow me." Because this call is issued by a living Lord, Jesus Christ, "the disciple's answer is not a spoken confession of faith in Jesus. Instead it is the obedient deed. . . . Christianity without the living Jesus Christ remains necessarily a Christianity without discipleship; and a Christianity without discipleship is always a Christianity without Jesus Christ. It is an idea, a myth."[78]

For Bonhoeffer, the response of the first disciples to immediately "leave all and follow Jesus" was not some idealistic image for subsequent followers to merely consider. Rather, it is a necessary response for all who heed the call of the living Lord. "Only the believers obey, and only the obedient believe. . . . Faith is possible only in this new state of existence created by obedience."[79] Bonhoeffer was critical of any doctrine that detaches following from faith, obedience from believing. Just as active obedience implies authentic faith, so authentic faith implies active obedience.

"Simple obedience" is the phrase that addresses the practicality of leaving all to follow Jesus. Bonhoeffer uses the biblical examples of Peter and the Rich Young Man to discuss the worldly demands and distractions that always accompany significant commitments. Yet, because the call of Jesus Christ is of utmost priority, reorganizing commitments and accepting the call can only lead to greater freedom and more authentic living.

Bonhoeffer makes clear that simple obedience to Jesus Christ implies a life of shared suffering.

> So Jesus has to make it clear and unmistakable to his disciples that the need to suffer now applies to them, too. Just as Christ is only Christ as one who suffers and is rejected, so a disciple is a disciple only in suffering and being rejected, thereby participating in crucifixion. Discipleship as allegiance to the person of Jesus Christ places the follower under the law of Christ, that is, under the cross. . . . Whenever Christ calls us, his call leads us to death.[80]

This yoking of discipleship and the cross has important implications for the proclamation of the church. Recently, mainline churches are experiencing a decline in membership, all the while wondering what is needed to reverse this trend and fill their pews again. It is extremely tempting to proclaim a gospel that offers blessing in the form of security and success. But where is the call to discipleship—yoked with suffering—about which Jesus preached and Bonhoeffer spoke? Certainly not in the bait and switch theology which says to people, "Follow the Lord for success and security—and only later, possibly, will we discuss suffering." It appears that many churches in America are peddling an "idea or myth"[81] of Christian redemption which lacks costly grace and authentic discipleship.

Suffering, for Dietrich Bonhoeffer, is not an unfortunate turn of events that might happen after a person is redeemed by Jesus Christ. Suffering is intrinsic to any life that has been baptized in Jesus Christ. Bonhoeffer's challenge to the church today is to always connect, and never detach, salvation *and* suffering that comes when we follow Jesus Christ. "Discipleship is being bound to the suffering Christ."[82]

With nearly a third of *Discipleship* devoted to the Sermon on the Mount, Bonhoeffer's thoughts on the Beatitudes remain some of the most inspiring and insightful words written on the subject:

> The disciples . . . are needy in every way. . . . They have no security, no property . . . no earthly community . . . neither spiritual power of their own. . . . For his sake they have lost all that . . . they mourn over the world, its guilt, its fate and its happiness . . . they bear suffering by the power of him who supports them . . . they are meek, who renounce all rights of their own for the sake of Jesus Christ. Those who now possess the earth with violence and injustice will lose it, and those who renounce it here, who were meek unto the cross, will rule over the new earth . . . even renouncing their own righteousness . . . they look forward to God's future righteousness . . . hungry and thirsty along the way . . . in the renunciation of their own dignity, for they are merciful. . . . Disciples give away anyone's greatest possession, their own dignity and honor, and show mercy. . . . Those who renounce their own good and evil . . . have purity of heart through the word of Jesus . . . they renounce violence and strife. . . . Jesus' disciples maintain peace by choosing to suffer instead of causing others to suffer . . . they renounce self-assertion and are silent in the face of hatred and injustice. That is how they overcome evil with good . . . suffering for the sake of a righteous cause. . . . Not recognition, but rejection, will be their reward from the world for their word and deed. . . . With him they lost everything, and with him they found everything.[83]

Bonding with Jesus Christ, Yet Breaking with the World

In the first part of *Discipleship*, Bonhoeffer lays the biblical foundation for bonding with Jesus Christ. Part two begins with the question, "How, then, does his call to discipleship reach us today?"

> Jesus no longer walks past me in bodily form and calls, "Follow me," as he did Levi, the tax collector. . . . If we want to hear his call to discipleship, we need to hear it where Christ himself is present. It is within the church that Jesus Christ calls through word and sacrament.[84]

Bonhoeffer understands that we become Christ's possession at our baptism. At the same time, we experience a break between past and present, between ourselves and the world. "I am deprived of my immediate relationship to the given realities of the world, since Christ the mediator and Lord has stepped inbetween me and the world. . . . The break with the world is absolute. . . . In baptism we die together with our old world."[85]

> This breaking with the immediacy of the world is nothing other than recognizing Christ as the Son of God, the mediator. . . . So people called by Jesus learn that they had lived an illusion in their relationship to the world. The illusion is immediacy. It has blocked faith and obedience. . . . Ever since Jesus called, there are no longer natural, historical, or experiential unmediated relationships for his disciples. . . . There is no way from us to others than the path through Christ, his word, and our following him. . . . there can be no unmediated relationships, even the most intimate ties of their lives, in the blood ties to father and mother, to children, brothers and sisters, in marital love, in historical responsibilities.[86]

Bonding with Jesus Christ breaks our immediate connection with the world. There still remains a person's love for, and life in, the world, but such love and life is always mediated through Jesus Christ. The disciple now sees the world through the eyes of Christ, understands the world with the mind of Christ, and feels the world with the heart of Christ. Any other seeing or thinking or feeling about the world is, for Bonhoeffer, illusion.

It may appear that this bonding with Jesus Christ and breaking with the world is not a very attractive package. The call to discipleship, which involves obedience and suffering, bonding and breaking, might seem rather masochistic. However, with this bonding and breaking comes mercy, joy, refreshment, and peace.

> Only Jesus Christ, who bids us follow him, knows where the path will lead. But we know that it will be a path full of mercy beyond measure. Discipleship is joy. . . . Bearing the cross does not bring misery and despair. Rather, it provides refreshment and peace for our souls; it is our greatest joy. . . . Under his yoke we are assured of his nearness and communion. It is he himself whom disciples find when they take up their cross.[87]

To be in nearness and communion with God in Jesus Christ is the reward of Christian discipleship. "We must not confuse free with cheap. It is free only in one sense, but it is quite costly in another. It will cost us our lives; however, in losing our lives, we gain life."[88]

It is worth mentioning that Bonhoeffer himself had a reservation regarding this book, as he revealed in a July 21, 1944, letter to Eberhard Bethge: "I thought I myself could learn to have faith by trying to live something like a saintly life. I suppose I wrote *Discipleship* at the end of this path. Today I clearly see the dangers of that book, though I still stand by it."[89] Because *Discipleship* is the most popular and widely read of Bonhoeffer's writings, many have offered opinions as to what exactly those "dangers" would be. Given Bonhoeffer's passionate emphasis on the importance of God's saving grace, some have wondered if *Discipleship*, with its emphasis on obedience, was just a detour.

> Did Bonhoeffer betray the Reformation by developing a new doctrine of sanctification? . . . He believes that justification by faith remains the incontestable presupposition and needs no supplement. But it needs reinstallation by the preservation of the costliness of the gift. *Discipleship* is an expression of that preservation, so badly needed to secure justification of the sinner over against the justification of sin.[90]

> I believe that the danger he referred to was not one of "works righteousness," that is, that we would try to justify ourselves before God by doing good works. Rather, it was that our efforts to lead a holy life of discipleship might lead us to be more interested in ourselves than in others. We might want to make something of ourselves rather than "being there for others."[91]

For Bonhoeffer, *Discipleship* remained very important, in spite of its possible dangers. Jesus' total claim on each disciple is compensated for by a bonding with Christ which creates joy, refreshment, peace. *Discipleship* is "the challenging call to the costly but joyful following of Jesus Christ in the modern world."[92]

CHAPTER FOUR

Ethics Is Conforming
to Jesus Christ,
Yet Reconnecting to the World

The first period of Dietrich Bonhoeffer's life, his academic period, served as his "foundation."[93] The second period, focusing on his ministry in the church, has been called a time of "concentration." In chapters four and five we now move into the third and final period, "liberation." It was in this period that Bonhoeffer wrote *Ethics* (1940-1943) and *Letters and Papers from Prison* (1943-1945).

There is a fundamental continuity throughout Bonhoeffer's life, even though his circumstances changed and his theology deepened. After writing *Life Together*, there was a "turning away from the 'churchly' formulation of the central themes of his theology and towards their restatement in a more 'worldly' form."[94]

"[W]hereas in *Discipleship* the emphasis was on the 'church against the world,' a church with clear-cut boundaries, in his *Ethics* the boundaries became more open. . . ."[95] Bonding with Jesus Christ evolved into conforming to Jesus Christ as Bonhoeffer moved from a narrow context of the "churchly" to a more expansive embrace of the "worldly."

In a fundamental, not fundamentalist, way, Bonhoeffer challenges us to frame our ethics not according to tradition (e.g. attempting to do good by using principles, trusting character, evaluating consequences, valuing situations), but by asking: What is the will of God?[96] Bonhoeffer knew very well the history of ethical deliberation, yet he argued radically for awareness of and conversation with the living presence of God in Jesus Christ. Principles can be helpful, character shapes persons, consequences keep us connected to reality, but all of these merely provide the context for responsible, free action based on obeying the living voice of Jesus Christ. Seeking to do God's will goes beyond the question of "good" and "evil" because that contrast already reveals a "falling away from the origin,"[97] He writes:

> The knowledge of good and evil appears to be the goal of all ethical reflection. The first task of Christian ethics is to supercede that knowledge. This attack on the presuppositions of all other ethics is so unique that it is questionable whether it even makes sense to speak of Christian ethics at all. If it is nevertheless done, then this can only mean that Christian ethics claims to articulate the origin of the whole ethical enterprise.[98]

It is good to remember that Bonhoeffer made this shift in ethical deliberation during the time of Nazi Germany, when evil was masqueraded as good and wrong was packaged as right. Bonhoeffer became convinced that discerning the right thing to do required more than simply employing traditional ethical formulas. The "rusty weapons"[99] of yesterday were not capable of combating the enemy he found himself facing. His fundamental approach for doing ethics would lie in returning to that place where God's will began and from which all responsible and free action ought to have its origin: Jesus Christ, the center!

Christ, Reality and Good

With the 1998 publication of *Ethik* in Germany, and the subsequent English edition of *Ethics* in 2005, Bonhoeffer's manuscript of "Christ, Reality and Good—Christ, Church and World" was placed at the beginning.[100] Here Bonhoeffer lays out the theological foundation for ethical deliberations:

But the will of God is nothing other than the realization of the Christ-reality among us and in our world. The will of God is therefore not an idea that demands to be realized; it is itself already reality in the self-revelation of God in Jesus Christ. The will of God . . . is a reality that wills to become real ever anew in what exists and against what exists. The will of God has already been fulfilled by God, in reconciling the world to himself in Christ. . . . Since the appearance of Christ, ethics can be concerned with only one thing: to participate in the reality of the fulfilled will of God.[101]

The "Christ-reality among us" has been fulfilled, but it needs to be realized. It is neither an idea that must be developed, nor a program that has been completed. It is "a reality that wills to become real ever anew in what exists and against what exists." Some have used the phrase "already, not yet" to speak about the kingdom of God. God has "already" inaugurated the kingdom in Israel and then in Jesus, but its fullness is "not yet" accomplished. We are still called to do the work of the kingdom, realizing that which is already real!

Bonhoeffer offers an image of how the church has traditionally viewed reality, an image of the world divided into two realms: "[T]wo realms bump against each other: one divine, holy, supernatural, and Christian; the other worldly, profane, natural, and unchristian. . . . Reality as a whole splits into two parts . . . [creating] the possibility of existence in only one of these sectors. . . .[we] are left with only the following options. Giving up on reality as a whole, we place ourselves in one of the two realms, wanting Christ without the world or the world without Christ."[102] Bonhoeffer declares that this is contrary to the New Testament, where the "whole reality of the world has already been drawn into and is held together in Christ."[103]

There are not two realities, but only one reality, and that is God's reality revealed in Christ in the reality of the world. Partaking in Christ, we stand at the same time in the reality of God and in the reality of the world. . . . Belonging completely to Christ, one stands at the same time completely in the world.[104]

Many people live, to some degree, with this dualistic worldview. Good should be affirmed while evil must be rejected; God is to be embraced while Satan is to be resisted. For many people, rejecting evil and resisting Satan are conscious and necessary activities, since the final outcome is undetermined. Bonhoeffer at no point minimizes evil, but he does reject a view of reality that questions the outcome: "I never experience the reality of God without the reality of the world, nor the reality of the world without the reality of God. . . . The world is not divided between Christ and the devil; it is completely the world of Christ, whether it be reconciled or not."[105]

Bonhoeffer's opening lines in this first segment of *Ethics* critique the two questions which traditionally shape ethical deliberations: How can I *be* good? and How can I *do* good? Instead, Bonhoeffer says, one must ask a completely different question: What is the will of God? "The question of the good becomes the question of participating in God's reality revealed in Christ. . . . Only by participating in reality do we also share in the good."[106] This "participating in reality" would later be Bonhoeffer's justification for his involvement in the resistance movement. It was not justified because of good intentions (most people have those), nor by its outcome (the July 20 plot failed). What made his conspiratorial activity necessary was that it was done responsibly while participating in one reality, in the one world, a world already reconciled to God in Jesus Christ.

Has Bonhoeffer, by affirming one worldly realm, undermined the necessity of the church? Not at all. In the middle of the opening section, "Christ, Reality and Good," Bonhoeffer attests to the importance, even indispensability, of the church as the living body of Christ:

[T]he space of the church is the place where witness is given to the foundation of all reality in Jesus Christ. The church is the place where it is proclaimed and taken seriously that God has reconciled the world to himself in Christ. . . . The space of the church is not there in order to fight with the world for a piece of its territory, but precisely to testify to the world that it is still the world, namely, the world that is loved and reconciled by God. . . . It desires no more space than it needs to serve the world with its witness to Jesus Christ and to the world's reconciliation to God through Jesus Christ.[107]

So the "churchly" is neither all important, nor is it unimportant. Rather, the church exists to witness that the entire world belongs to God! Bonhoeffer's Christology requires that disciples reconnect with the world because that is precisely where "Christ, reality and good" come together.

The Structure of Responsible Life

The structure of responsible life is determined in a two-fold manner, namely, by life's bond to human beings and to God, and by the freedom of one's own life. . . . [W]ithout this bond and without this freedom there can be no responsibility.[108]

Specifically, life's "bond and freedom" are expanded in *Ethics* through four concepts: vicarious representative action, accordance with reality, taking on guilt, and freedom.[108] These four concepts describe the structure of responsible life for those who are conformed to Jesus Christ and connected to the world. These concepts 1) provide concrete help for persons who strive to live responsibly in the world, and 2) reflect the life of Jesus Christ, to whom such persons conform. The life of Jesus Christ was one of vicarious representative action (life for others), in accordance with reality (harsh, crucifying reality), taking on guilt (the sins of the world), and freedom (his journey to Jerusalem). A disciple's life, bonded to Jesus Christ, will inevitably assume the same structure.

First, "vicarious representative action," an important concept in Bonhoeffer's ethics, was already present in his doctoral dissertation when he spoke of responsibility in community.[110] Later, in *Letters and Papers from Prison*, vicarious representative action resurfaced in the powerful admonition of life lived for others. "Vicarious representative action, and therefore responsibility, is possible only in completely devoting one's own life to another person."[111] Responsible life is always shaped by a passion to live and die for others.

The second concept, "in accordance with reality," is again Christological; responsible life in accordance with reality is centered on Jesus Christ, the "Real One." Neither the expedient, successful, or status quo is reality, nor the protest, rebellion, or rejected. That alone which is "in and from Jesus Christ" is in accordance with reality. He is the origin, essence, and goal of all reality, who has loved, judged, and reconciled the world.

Third, "taking on guilt" is a concept rich in meaning, yet superficially at odds with most human religiosity. Does not the sacrifice of Jesus Christ on Calvary remove the consequence of sin and eliminate the burden of guilt? Why would disciples of Jesus then take on more guilt? Yet, because discipleship is conforming to Jesus Christ, the one who is bonded to him will necessarily experience a life which is "guilty yet sinless."[112] What Bonhoeffer feels is important is not that a person labors to maintain his or her own innocence from sin, but rather, like Jesus, to share and bear the sin and brokenness of others. Taking on guilt relates intimately with vicarious representative action, as the one bonded to Jesus Christ willingly shares the burdens of others. This notion was further developed in Bonhoeffer's prison reflections, when he recalls a conversation with a friend:

We had simply asked ourselves what we really
wanted to do with our lives . . . if one has completely renounced making something of oneself . . .
then one throws oneself completely into the arms of
God . . . then one takes seriously no longer one's
own sufferings [and sin] but rather the suffering of
God in the world.[113]

For Bonhoeffer, taking on guilt by being responsible for
others is a necessary component of bonding with Jesus Christ,
in a life lived for others.

Fourth, "freedom" is a necessary aspect of responsibility and
a key to any life bonded to Jesus Christ. Of course, this begs the
question of the relation between free responsibility and obedience.[114] Bonhoeffer understands these two elements are related to
and reflective of Jesus Christ himself. "Jesus stands before God as
the obedient one and as the free one. . . . Obedience binds
freedom, freedom ennobles obedience. . . . Freedom dares to act
and leaves the judgment about good and evil up to God."[115]
There is an inner tension between obedience and freedom, and
accepting both is the key to responsible discipleship.

In a critique of mere duty, Bonhoeffer reinforces the truth and
necessity of freedom: "[T]hose who limit themselves to duty will
never venture a free action that rests solely on their own responsibility, the only sort of action that can meet evil at its heart and
overcome it. People of duty must finally fulfill their duty even to
the devil."[116] It was the concept of responsible freedom that
undergirded Bonhoeffer and the conspirators when planning
the assassination of Hitler. Conversely, it was blind duty that
paralyzed many other Germans from acting against genocide
being perpetrated against the Jews and other "undesirables."
"Only a Christian who understands that he or she is free can
make the right ethical decisions."[117] This dynamic tension of
freedom and obedience is more fully discussed in relation to the
conspiracy in *Dietrich Bonhoeffer: Reality and Resistance*, by
ethicist and Bonhoeffer scholar, Larry Rasmussen. [118]

Before concluding, it is important to highlight one final pair of ideas that further amplify Bonhoeffer's passion to connect the reality of God and the reality of the world. In a section of *Ethics* entitled "Ultimate and Penultimate Things,"[119] he speaks about the proper relationship between the ultimate reality of God (justification and reconciliation) and the penultimate realities of the world (history, brokenness, conflict). He identifies radicalism and compromise as two extreme, but wrong, ways to resolve the tension inherent between these two realities. "Radicalism always arises from a conscious or unconscious hatred of what exists. . . . Compromise always arises from hatred of the ultimate . . . both attitudes are equally opposed to Christ."[120] God, in Jesus Christ, has loved, affirmed, and reconciled the world, giving the penultimate reality importance and meaning. Bonhoeffer knew that God's ultimate word of justification and reconciliation is most important, yet "there are situations that make it harder or easier to have faith."[121] He used the penultimate example of feeding the hungry as a way of preparing the "way for the coming of grace."[122]

As *Discipleship* was conceived and written during the early years of National Socialism in Germany, with the church's struggle as the immediate context for bonding with Jesus Christ yet breaking with the world, *Ethics* is the journal that describes Bonhoeffer's reconnecting with the world while conforming to Jesus Christ, all within the context of conspiring to assassinate Hitler. In a very deep and disciplined way, he reflects on what it means to love God and the world through the life, love, and lens of Jesus Christ. "Bonhoeffer never wrote in the abstract,"[123] and such concrete engagement is part of what makes his writings ever relevant. The Holocaust called into question all traditional ways of thinking about good and evil, and Bonhoeffer's Christ-centered reflections during that chaotic time can be very helpful in our ethical deliberations.

CHAPTER FIVE

Worldly Christianity Is Standing by God, Yet Living for Others

Dietrich Bonhoeffer's life as a Lutheran pastor, a university professor, and a conspirator came to a halt on April 5, 1943, when he was arrested and taken to Tegel Military Prison in Northwest Berlin. The charge against him was "subversion of the armed forces." On the same day, his brother-in-law, Hans von Dohnanyi, was arrested for being an "initiator and intellectual leader of the movement for removal of the *Führer*," and his sister, Christine (von Dohnanyi's wife), was taken for "aiding high treason." She was released April 30 and survived the war, but Hans and Dietrich remained imprisoned until their deaths on April 9, 1945. The arrests of Dietrich Bonhoeffer and Hans von Dohnany, and later Klaus Bonhoeffer and Dietrich's brother-in-law, Rüdiger Schleicher, began a painful chapter for the Bonhoeffer family as they struggled to survive war-torn Germany while facing the potential loss of four immediate family members.

During the first year of his imprisonment, Bonhoeffer waited for his trial, after which he expected to be released from prison. The loneliness and anxiety of solitary confinement was balanced only by the hope of eventually returning to his former life. He read the Moravian *Losungen* daily to find comfort, memories of earlier days with his family and at Finkenwalde. It was during this first year at Tegel Prison that he experimented with writing fiction, an effort he later abandoned, but not before compiling what would become *Fiction from Tegel Prison.*[124] As the months of imprisonment wore on, Bonhoeffer was allowed to correspond with his parents, his siblings, and his fiancée, Maria. Seven and one-half months after his arrest, he began writing to his best friend, Eberhard Bethge, thanks to the help of Corporal Knobloch, a sympathetic prison guard.

In a letter dated April 11, 1944, he wrote, "I have been told not to expect any change in my current situation for the time being."[125] This discouraging news came on the heels of his interrogation by the Reich War Court and made him feel for the first time that he might not be released. It was this sober realization that, in part, stimulated Bonhoeffer's deeper theological reflections and subsequent letters to Eberhard Bethge. While the "Tegel [family] letters became the elixir of life for Bonhoeffer,"[126] the "theological letters" would become the primary reason the wider world would come to know him. Specifically, his letters to Bethge on April 30, May 5 and 29, June 8, July 16, 18, and 21 contain his reflections about a "world come of age," the "non-religious interpretations of biblical concepts," and living life "with God [yet] without God." *Letters and Papers from Prison* is truly a Christian classic.[127]

Letters and Papers from Prison is the primary source of information about Bonhoeffer's two years in prison.[128] The critical edition of this 750-page masterpiece was released in 2010, and, like the other volumes in the *Dietrich Bonhoeffer Works*, it is the product of an international team of scholars, the result of almost five decades of research and reflection.

After publishing Bonhoeffer's *Ethics* in 1949, Bethge decided that the letters and papers from Bonhoeffer that he still had in his desk should be shared, and so the first edition of *Widerstand und Ergebung* (Resistance and Submission) was issued in 1951. Two years later the first English translation was printed as *Letters and Papers from Prison*.[129]

Conspiracy and Imprisonment 1940-1945 (DBWE 16) is also "an essential companion volume to Bonhoeffer's writings from the war years: *Ethics* (DBWE 6), *Fiction from Tegel Prison* (DBWE 7), and *Letters and Papers from Prison* (DBWE 8)."[130] Primarily correspondence, essays, and notes, *Conspiracy and Imprisonment 1940-1945* provides significant contextual detail for better understanding the final years of Bonhoeffer's life. *Love Letters from Cell 92: The Correspondence Between Dietrich Bonhoeffer and Maria von Wedemeyer 1943-45* is also helpful in understanding his relationship with Maria during this same time.[131]

In 2011, a monograph was written that tells the story of *Letters and Papers from Prison*. The eminently qualified church historian, Martin E. Marty, who first wrote about Bonhoeffer in 1962,[132] accepted the invitation from Princeton University Press to write *Dietrich Bonhoeffer's Letters and Papers from Prison: A Biography*[133] as part of Princeton University Press's new series, Lives of Great Religious Books. Marty traces the "reception, interpretation, and influence" of *Letters and Papers from Prison*, showing how it still remains a "living thing" today.

It is easy to see why the reflections of Dietrich Bonhoeffer while imprisoned by the Nazis not only stimulated interest in his work, but also heavily influenced twentieth-century and twenty-first-century Christian theology. In his April 30, 1943, letter to Bethge, Bonhoeffer wrote:

> What might surprise or perhaps even worry you would be my theological thoughts and where they are leading, and here is where I really miss you very much. I don't know anyone else with whom I can talk about them and arrive at some clarity. What keeps gnawing at me is the question, what is Christianity, or who is Christ actually for us today? . . .

We are approaching a completely religionless age; people as they are now simply cannot be religious anymore. . . . How can Christ become Lord of the religionless as well? Is there such a thing as a religionless Christian?. . . Religious people speak of God at a point where human knowledge is at an end . . . or when human strength fails. . . . I'd like to speak of God not at the boundaries but in the center, not in weakness but in strength, thus not in death and guilt but in human life and human goodness.[134]

Five days later he wrote: "What does it mean to 'interpret religiously?' . . . It means, in my opinion, to speak metaphysically, on the one hand, and on the other hand, individualistically. Neither way is appropriate, either for the biblical message or for people today."[135]

In these first of the "theological" letters, Bonhoeffer shares with Bethge his observation that religion, when seen as an individual human activity only to be exercised in times of dire need, is not an authentic form of Christian faith. Saving one's soul . . ."[136] was no longer a concern of many people, and focusing only on the next world seemed an insult to the God known in the incarnation of Jesus Christ. He acknowledged his theological mentor, Karl Barth, as one who had begun "thinking along these lines,"[137] yet he did not think Barth went far enough in his critique of religion. Specifically, Bonhoeffer criticized religion's attachment to "metaphysics and individualism."[138] Drawing from his thoughts in *The Communion of Saints* and the *Christology* lectures, he suggested that Christian faith is to be lived at the center of life (not at the metaphysical boundaries of the universe) and is to be communal in essence (not essentially private).

In his letter of May 29, he addressed the tendency of religious people to think of God as the filler of "gaps," the one who answers the questions and fixes the problems human knowledge cannot:

It has again brought home to me quite clearly that we shouldn't think of God as the stopgap [*Lückenbüßer*] for the incompleteness of our knowledge, because then—as is objectively inevitable—when the boundaries of knowledge are pushed ever further, God too is pushed further away and thus is ever on the retreat. We should find God in what we know, not in what we don't know; God wants to be grasped by us not in unsolved questions but in those that have been solved.[139]

This echoes his thoughts from 1933, that God—in Christ—is to be experienced at the center of "humanity, history, and nature."[140] Here, however, Bonhoeffer's idea on God's centrality is not theoretically abstract, but practical as he discovered that the centrality of God's presence was necessary if people of faith were ever to oppose Hitler. He wanted people to recognize God "in the midst of our lives, in life and not only in dying, in health and strength and not only in suffering, in action and not only in sin."[141]

In his June 8 letter, Bonhoeffer introduced the concept of the "world come of age" (*die Mündige Welt*).[142] He had been reading Wilhelm Dilthey's *Weltanschauung und Analyse*, in which not only science had matured, but also religion, law, and government. Bonhoeffer observed that the "universal human questions . . . are being answered 'without God.'"[143] He recommended that the church not attempt to "save some room for religion in the world"[144] or preserve the God-of-the-gaps. Bonhoeffer believed on the deepest level that life with Jesus Christ should be a mature life lived at the center of our world—in life, health, strength, and action. His respect for science, technology, and human autonomy was already ingrained, thanks to the influence of his agnostic-scientific father and brothers. He wrote, "The question is Christ and the world that has come of age."[145]

If there is a place in Bonhoeffer's *Letters and Papers from Prison* from which the "death of God" movement in the 1960s took root and caused conservative Christians to reject his theology, it is likely here.[146] Four days before the failed attempt to assassinate Hitler, Bonhoeffer spoke of more and more people living *etsi deus non daretur* (as if there were no God).[147]

> God would have us know that we must live as those who manage their lives without God. The same God who is with us is the God who forsakes us (Mark 15:34). The same God who makes us to live in the world without the working hypothesis of God is the God before whom we stand continually. Before God, and with God, we live without God. God consents to be pushed out of the world and onto the cross; God is weak and powerless in the world and in precisely this way, and only so, is at our side and helps us (Matthew 8:17). . . . Human religiosity directs people in need to the power of God in the world, God as *deus ex machina*. The Bible directs people toward the powerlessness and suffering of God; only the suffering God can help."[148]

Bonhoeffer understood that often when people feel helpless and out of control they reach for the power of God to come to their aid. The *deus ex machina* (literally, God of the machine) refers to a mechanical device used in the ancient Greek theatre by which gods could swoop down and rescue people in perilous situations. Religious people at times picture God this way, as one who can be invoked in situations where human powers fail. Bonhoeffer does not agree that this is the God known in Jesus Christ.

The letter "g" has been responsible for much of the confusion regarding the supposed absence of God of which Bonhoeffer speaks. The line reads: "Before God, and with God, we live without God."[149] It would be better, perhaps, to lowercase the last "God," which would then read, "Before God, and with God, we live without god." "Walking the path that Jesus walks . . . sharing in God's suffering in the worldly life"[150] is to live "before God and with God." We must do this without invoking a god of power, rescue, security, or success. Without desperately grasping for that false god of rescue, we are called to live with the true God of loving service.

The "death of God" proponents of the 1960s used this phrase ("we live without God") to promote the end of traditional theistic belief. Instead of seeing this as a misrepresentation of Bonhoeffer, which it certainly was, conservative Christians dismissed his reflections as undermining orthodox Christian theology. The ideas of his "theological" letters must be read and understood within the total trajectory of his theology from 1927 to 1945.

Bonhoeffer's final "theological" letter is that of July 21, 1944, the day after the failed plot on Hitler's life. In this letter, he sums up his life, his theology, and his faith with words filled with credibility and authenticity:

> I am still discovering to this day, that one only learns to have faith by living in the full this-worldliness of life . . . one throws oneself completely into the arms of God and this is what I call this-worldliness: living fully in the midst of life's tasks, questions, successes and failures, experiences and perplexities—then one takes seriously no longer one's own sufferings but rather the suffering of God in the world . . . this is how one becomes a human being, a Christian.[151]

Here he speaks of the meaning of this-worldliness, the essence of mature Christianity, while simultaneously criticizing human religiosity, which often focuses too much on a person's own suffering. Eberhard Bethge kept this letter in his possession until his death in 2000. It was his favorite letter from Bonhoeffer.[152] In its closing lines, Bethge sensed the depth of faith expressed by his best friend, the faith of one bonded with Jesus Christ, and therefore one who suffered in the world: "May God lead us kindly through these times, but above all, may God lead us to himself."[153]

Standing by God

In *Letters and Papers from Prison*, the pieces "After Ten Years"[154] and "Outline for a Book"[155] describe how "standing by God" also means "living for others."

"After Ten Years" was written for Christmas 1942, three and one-half months before Bonhoeffer was arrested and imprisoned. Bethge believed this piece connected Bonhoeffer's final days of freedom with his imprisonment. In it Bonhoeffer asks questions and offers suggestions on how his fellow conspirators ought to view all that had happened since Hitler was first appointed chancellor of the Reich on January 30, 1933. "In the following pages I want to try to give an accounting of some of the shared experience and insights that have been forced upon us in these times . . . conclusions about human experience . . . that have been reached together in a circle of like-minded people."[156] After beginning with the statement that they had "little ground under their feet," he rhetorically asks, "Who stands firm?" His answer: not persons with the greatest intellect, firm principles, solid consciences, private virtues, but rather, "one who is prepared to sacrifice all of these when, in faith and in relationship with God alone, he is called to obedient and responsible action."[157] He goes on to critique the "civil courage (*qua duty*)" that Germans had learned all too well, supporting instead "free responsible action" as the needed response. He encourages his fellow conspirators not to despise humanity, but to regard others in terms of what they suffer. He spoke of sympathy, suffering, and remaining optimistic, rhetorically asking whether they were "still of any use."

These reflections offer an honest, deep, even confessional way of viewing past and present. Bonhoeffer helped clarify what his colleagues were experiencing, offering divine perspective and support. He was convinced that as long as they acted responsibly and gave freely of themselves to others, they were "standing by God."

> It remains an experience of incomparable value that we have for once learned to see the great events of world history from below, from the perspective of the outcasts, the suspects, the maltreated, the powerless, the oppressed and reviled, in short from the perspective of the suffering. If only during this time bitterness and envy have not corroded the heart; that we come to see matters great and small, happiness and misfortune, strength and weakness with new eyes; that our sense for greatness, humanness, justice, and mercy has grown clearer, freer, more incorruptible; that we learn, indeed, that personal suffering is a more useful key, a more fruitful principle than personal happiness for exploring the meaning of the world in contemplation and action.[158]

There are times when doing something for others is impossible, and the best one can do is to stand by and suffer with them. This was especially true for Bonhoeffer during his imprisonment. The third verse of his poem, "Stations on the Way to Freedom" (August 1944), reflects such a time and place of suffering:

> Wondrous transformation. Your hands, strong and active, are fettered. Powerless, alone, you see that an end is put to your action. Yet now you breathe a sigh of relief and lay what is righteous calmly and fearlessly into a mightier hand, contented. Just for one blissful moment you could feel the sweet touch of freedom, then you gave it to God, that God might perfect it in glory.[159]

Living for Others

Also during the summer of 1944, Bonhoeffer wrote an outline for a book intended to be no more than 100 pages with three chapters. In it, he writes about humanity's coming of age, Christian faith, and the essence of the church. Two phrases from that outline summarize his convictions: "Faith is participating in this being of Jesus," and "The church is church only when it exists for others." Although slightly different, "participating in this being of Jesus" is similar to Bonhoeffer's earlier ideas of bonding with and conforming to Jesus Christ found in *Discipleship and Ethics*. "The church existing for others" is reminiscent of the "vicarious representative action" mentioned earlier in *The Communion of Saints*.[160]

Certainly all of Bonhoeffer's poems from prison deserve attention and close examination, but the one that seems most to capture his Christ-centered faith of "standing by God and living for others" is "Christians and Pagans," written in the summer of 1944.

> People go to God when they are sore bestead,*
> begging God for succor, wanting peace and daily bread.
> That they might be saved from sickness, freed from
>   sin and death,
> Christians, like all others, ask that God would be
>   their stead.
>
> We are called to find the places God is sore bestead,
> in our poor, neglected neighbors without home or bread.
> Overcome by grief God bears all sin and pain and death.
> Christians are to stand by God and suffer in God's stead.
>
> God goes out to ev'ry one when sore bestead,
> feeding bodies, spirits, offering the living bread.
> Christians, like all others, loved by God who hangs
>   there dead,
> offering, forgiving, sacrificing in their stead.

bestead = situated.

Worldly Christianity

"Worldly Christianity" captures the essence of Bonhoeffer's reflections from prison, and can even summarize his entire theology. From his father's love of science, in his family's passion for art and music, through the richness of personal relationships, and to his mature theology of living for others, Bonhoeffer's world affirming passion is evident. For him, Jesus Christ was not a religious redeemer who provided a way to escape this world for the next. Rather, Jesus Christ came to enlist all of humanity to do his work within the world. God created the world to love the world, and a person's "standing by God" is authenticated by "living for others." Worldly Christianity is Bonhoeffer's antidote to otherworldly/escapist religiosity.

As the church ponders Bonhoeffer's theology today, there are two questions to consider. First, has the world matured as Bonhoeffer conjectured? Was he primarily observing a mature world in Europe that experienced the fruit of the Enlightenment mentality, with its consequent growth of science and technology, as positively seen through the eyes and experience of his erudite family in early twentieth century Berlin? For many, especially in the developing world, Bonhoeffer's "world come of age" is nowhere close to their reality. Perhaps Dietrich Bonhoeffer was only speaking about his own world. Does this mean that only a part of the world has matured or is capable of maturity?

Second, there is evidence that many people are finding the traditional dogmas and doctrines of Christian faith hard to accept and follow; mainline churches are declining in membership. Yet, significant evidence also points to a revival of spirituality, even if it is not institutional religion per se. While some people resonate with Bonhoeffer's thoughts about religionlessness, others seem to be attracted to traditional expressions and experiences of religion.

Bonhoeffer thought that this tendency toward religionlessness was inevitable and far-reaching. Time will tell whether he was right. At any rate, it appears to be happening much more slowly than he predicted. Maturity and religionlessness were for Bonhoeffer key elements of authentic Christian faith. The enduring and important question is whether his reflections and impulses resonate with us and prompt us to more authentic Christian faith. Do the ideas of "standing by God" and "living for others" assist us in living out our faith in and with Jesus Christ? Is worldly Christianity something we can affirm?

CHAPTER SIX

Bonhoeffer's Enduring Legacy, Yet Challenging Issues

As Dietrich Bonhoeffer's career unfolds, one can observe in his life a faith that is authentic and a theology which has integrity. I believe that this faith and this theology are what constitute his enduring legacy. Faith that is authentic comes when one's beliefs and one's actions correspond with each other. The opposite of hypocrisy, authenticity describes a person's faith that is genuine, truthful, and ultimately transparent. Without doubt the authentic faith of Dietrich Bonhoeffer is most powerfully revealed in the sacrifice of his life for God and country. Bonhoeffer's martyrdom is most often what causes people to stand up and take notice of him, usually before they ever learn about his theology. Whether or not one agrees with Bonhoeffer that taking part in the plot to kill Hitler was the right thing to do, one cannot doubt that for him such a decision brought together his inner convictions and his outward actions. He is not only genuine and truthful, but ultimately transparent as his inner convictions shine through his outer actions. For Dietrich Bonhoeffer to have believed in the love and mercy of God in Jesus Christ for all of humanity, have been aware of the ongoing genocide in Nazi Germany, and then have refused to take action that possibly could end the evil, would have been for him inauthentic. At risk to his own life, he acted on his beliefs, and in that lies the authenticity of his faith.

Theology which has integrity results when persons of authentic faith honestly embrace the changing face of reality. For theology to avoid becoming stagnant and irrelevant, it needs to move beyond the simple uttering of beliefs and preservation of dogma, rather integrating beliefs and dogma with an ever-changing world, all under the lordship of Jesus Christ. One of the most dynamic elements of Bonhoeffer's enduring legacy is his desire to engage the world, in all its complexity and ambiguity, rather than diminish or dismiss it. Whereas religion too often hides behind static and outdated beliefs to defend itself against the world, faith that is authentic and theology with integrity embraces and engages God's ever-changing world. The integrity of Bonhoeffer's theology lay in his passion to integrate God's Word and God's world.

While faith and theology, characterized by authenticity and integrity, forever will be significant parts of Bonhoeffer's enduring legacy, one additional contribution reflects and reinforces his faith and theology—ecumenical vision. From his student days on, Bonhoeffer took part in ecumenical gatherings as often as possible, offering theological depth to discussions concerning the witness of the church. He had a passion for proclaiming the lordship of Jesus Christ for all humanity. At a time when most German Christians—and theologians—were focused on a more nationalistic understanding of the church, he lifted up the universal fellowship of those gathered around Jesus Christ. What occasioned his interest in ecumenical relations when most in European churches focused inward? No doubt Bonhoeffer's relationships with "others" shaped his more universal orientation of Christian faith; likely, his ongoing involvement with Christians outside his own country prevented him from ever thinking that German Christians were the preferred recipients of God's love and blessing. His vicarage in Barcelona, his visits to Rome, his parish involvement in Harlem, his friendship with French pacifist Jean Lasserre, his first-hand conversations with Scandinavian Lutherans, and his close association with English Bishop George Bell, to name only the most obvious, all helped create an appreciation of the universality of the church. His ability to critique Germany's domestication of the Gospel was largely a result of his personal experiences of the church universal. While his theology offered the substance for his ecumenical vision, his relationships with "others" around the world provided him the inspiration. The Christ-centered faith, theology, and ecumenicity of Dietrich Bonhoeffer will likely remain key to his enduring legacy.

Bonhoeffer himself would likely say that any enduring legacy should include challenging issues. There appear to be at least four in Bonhoeffer's life and work.

First, an apparent dissonance surfaces because this Lutheran pastor (who at an earlier time was a committed pacifist) became involved in a plot to murder a head of state. For some, Bonhoeffer's involvement in the July 20 plot to assassinate Adolf Hitler inspires deep respect; for others, it appears to contradict his Christian faith because it directly violates the strict prohibition against murder in the Ten Commandments. For this reason, some dismiss him as misguided, though sincere. However, this apparent contradiction is best understood when we consider its context. Bonhoeffer was well aware, through information he received from his brother-in-law, Hans von Dohnanyi, in the Reich Ministry of Justice, that the Nazis were murdering thousands of innocent people every day; to do nothing was to be somehow complicit in the ongoing genocide. He also knew that only the removal of such a tyrannical leader could possibly end the Nazi's reign of terror. Assassinating Adolf Hitler would save hundreds of thousands of lives at the cost of one. Bonhoeffer did believe that killing even one person was wrong, yet allowing the slaughter of thousands was exponentially worse. He was keenly aware that his actions would be perceived by many as unpatriotic, but his commitment was to the Lord of life, not the pseudo-messiah, Adolf Hitler. He firmly believed that his complicity was, in fact, more patriotic than unquestioning obedience. Might his life inspire ours in ethically gray areas that require bold, risky decisions?

A second challenging issue in Bonhoeffer's enduring legacy is his attitude toward Jews and Judaism.[161] The Bonhoeffers were uncommonly open-minded in their attitude towards Jews. They lived with Jewish neighbors in the Grünewald district of Berlin, and it is no surprise that some of Bonhoeffer's close friends were Jewish. There is no question that everyone in the Bonhoeffer family had a fundamental aversion to the Nazi's anti-Semitism. However, Bonhoeffer was not immune to traditional Christian supercessionism.[162] Bonhoeffer's views on this subject are ambiguous in some of his teaching and preaching,[163] while his life and sacrifice portray equality and acceptance.

The question is whether Bonhoeffer's more traditional views would have evolved over time, especially in light of post-Holocaust awareness and sensitivities. Does his deep conviction about the centrality (superiority?) of Jesus Christ not only in the church, but for humanity, history, and nature allow room for serious interfaith dialogue? While any respectful conversation about ultimate things understands that "the truth is bigger than both of us,"[164] Bonhoeffer was quite confident that his particular conviction about the centrality of Jesus Christ was absolutely true and, given that confidence, viewing Jews as equals in theological dialogue would appear challenging. It is Bonhoeffer's early statements about Jews and Judaism that have prevented him from being recognized as a "Righteous Among the Nations" at the Holocaust Martyrs and Heroes Remembrance Authority in Jerusalem.[165]

A third issue is whether Bonhoeffer ought to be designated as a Christian martyr.[166] Did Bonhoeffer die for the Lord of his faith or did he perish in the ashes of the Third Reich simply, though unselfishly, as a "good German"? This issue was discussed soon after the war ended, as cities re-named streets after those who died bearing heroic witness. When the name of Dietrich Bonhoeffer was suggested for such an honor, one pastor discouraged it because he did not "want the names of our colleagues, who were killed for their faith, lumped together with political martyrs."[167] For that pastor, Christian martyrdom is distinct from political resistance. Bonhoeffer's father responded that, while Dietrich would not think himself worthy of such an honor, he certainly would not have distinguished himself from his fellow conspirators during those times. The distinction this pastor made would not have been shared by Bonhoeffer, whose life and sacrifice was Christ-centered—in, with, and under the tainted ambiguity of political, military history. If bearing witness to Jesus Christ includes responsible deeds done for others, then Bonhoeffer and some of his colleagues in the resistance deserve the designation of Christian martyr.

In the list of Lesser Festivals and Commemorations for *Evangelical Lutheran Worship,* Dietrich Bonhoeffer's name is followed by the designation "theologian." The name of Martin Luther King Jr. is followed by the designation "renewer of society, martyr." Martin Luther King Jr. was a victim of a violent crime, a person thoroughly committed to non-violent resistance. But how about Bonhoeffer, who died because he participated in a military conspiracy to murder a head of state? To argue that King died as an innocent victim, whereas Bonhoeffer was murdered because of his own complicity in tyrannicide, is to misunderstand both the nature of their deeds and the essence of their faith. Both men lived Christ-centered lives, and both men saw the political arena as a responsible place for God's activity. Insofar as Dietrich Bonhoeffer died for the sake of Jesus Christ, responsibly acting on behalf of others, is he not a Christian martyr?

On July 8, 1998, a service of commemoration and dedication was held at Westminster Abbey in London as ten statues were placed in niches above the west entrance. The ten martyrs of the twentieth century placed there included Martin Luther King Jr. and Dietrich Bonhoeffer.[168] That Anglicans at Westminster unanimously declared Bonhoeffer a martyr while

Lutherans in America still have their doubts testifies to the challenging legacy Bonhoeffer has left behind.

A fourth point of contention in Bonhoeffer's work has to do with his views on the role of women. Renate Bethge, Eberhard's wife, became playfully critical of Dietrich's traditional, patriarchal view of marriage, although she understood that such a view was widely accepted in their time. Lisa E. Dahill writes: "Patriarchy in Bonhoeffer does not represent merely another 'issue'; it undermines his entire analysis of the self and its spiritual formation."[169] In a similar way, Andras Csepregi writes about this issue in "Gender Inequality as a Basic Conviction Behind Bonhoeffer's Theology."[170] Bonhoeffer's ideas about this particular topic confirm that he was a man of his time and not immune to the prevailing attitudes and cultural stereotypes that he inherited. One could guess that Bonhoeffer would most likely later have rejected these stereotypes, especially considering the success of his fiancée, Maria von Wedemeyer, as an executive with Honeywell Corporation.

Additional Fragments of Bonhoeffer's Enduring Legacy

On June 15, 1930, Bonhoeffer gave an inspiring "Eulogy for Adolf von Harnack" at his neighbor's funeral. While at Union Seminary in 1930, he keenly observed—and then wrote—that America seemed to have "Protestantism without Reformation." To a Protestant Continuing Education Institute for Women in Potsdam-Hermannswerder on November 19, 1932, Bonhoeffer delivered "Thy Kingdom Come! The Prayer of the Church-Community for God's Kingdom on Earth." Before an ecumenical conference in Fanø, Denmark, in August 1934, he delivered an electrifying speech titled "The Church and the People of the World" in which he stated, "Peace is the opposite of security." In early 1943, Bonhoeffer sent two touching sermons from prison: a wedding sermon for Eberhard and Renate Bethge and a baptismal sermon for his godson and namesake, Dietrich Bethge. While in prison, he also wrote the poems, "Stations on the Way to Freedom," "The Friend," "By Powers of Good," and "Who Am I?" to name only a few.

Any person whose words and actions continue to instruct and inspire others long after their death must be counted among the great cloud of witnesses sent by God. Dietrich Bonhoeffer continues to inspire and instruct scores of people who, through his convictions and contradictions, see reflections of God's love and justice. May we, through our words and actions, our convictions and contradictions, also share God's love and work for God's justice. May our conforming to Jesus Christ reconnect us to the world, a world already reconciled to God, still waiting to be made real in our lives. May we experience worldly Christianity as we stand by God and live for others.

Soli Deo Gloria!

Chronology

1906 Dietrich Bonhoeffer is born in Breslau, Germany (now Wrocław, Poland), on February 4

1912 Bonhoeffer family moves to Berlin

1918 Brother Walter killed in WWI

1923 Begins studies at the University of Tübingen

1924 Transfers to Kaiser Wilhelm University in Berlin

1927 Completes doctorate with dissertation, *The Communion of Saints*

1928 Serves one year as assistant pastor in Barcelona, Spain

1929 Takes position as academic assistant to Professor Wilhelm Lütgert in Berlin

1930 Qualifies as university teacher (with *Habilitation* thesis, "Act and Being"); accepts one-year Sloan Fellowship to study at Union Theological Seminary in New York City

1931 Ordained on November 15; teaches at Technical University and conducts confirmation classes; appointed youth secretary of the World Alliance Conference in Cambridge; meets Karl Barth in Bonn; begins university teaching in systematic theology

1932 Attends ecumenical meetings in Switzerland, Czechoslovakia, and Germany

1933 Hitler appointed chancellor on January 30; Aryan legislation soon follows; boycott of Jewish businesses on April 1; Bonhoeffer begins work with Martin Niemöller and the Pastors' Emergency League, works on Bethel Confession; in October called to serve two congregations in London

1934   Confessing Church founded out of the Synod of
        Barmen; Bonhoeffer attends the Fanø Ecumenical
        Conference; Hitler consolidates positions of Reich
        president and Reich chancellor into one Reich *Führer*
        when Hindenburg dies

1935   Departs England in April to direct Confessing Church
        Seminary at Finkenwalde

1936   Travels with students to Scandinavia; attends Chamby
        Conference in Switzerland; teaching permit revoked in
        August by the Reich Ministry of Education

1937   Martin Niemöller arrested and imprisoned;
        Finkenwalde closed by the Gestapo; begins collective
        pastorates in Kösslin and Gross-Schlönwitz; *Disciple-
        ship* published

1938   Begins contact with Oster and Canaris regarding
        military resistance to Hitler; writes *Life Together* in
        Göttingen following the emigration of his sister
        Sabine's family to England

1939   Leaves in June for America, but returns in July; applies
        for military chaplaincy

1940   Collective pastorates closed by the Gestapo; meets with
        Oster and Dohnanyi regarding employment by military
        counter intelligence (*Abwehr*); assigned to Munich
        office; forbidden to speak in public and required to
        report regularly to police; begins writing *Ethics*

1941   Travels for *Abwehr* to Switzerland; assists group of
        Jews to escape (Operation Seven)

1942   Travels for *Abwehr* to Norway and Sweden; has
        conversations with the Vatican

1943   Becomes engaged to Maria von Wedemeyer; failed
        assassination plots on Hitler (March 13 and 21);
        arrested on April 5 and taken to Tegel Military Prison,
        Berlin

1944   Waiting for trial with hopes of release, writes *Letters
        and Papers from Prison;* July 20 assassination plot
        against Hitler fails; moves to Prinz Albrecht Strasse

jail after evidence found regarding the resistance movement; brother, Klaus, and brother-in-law, Rüdiger, imprisoned

1945   Transferred to Buchenwald, Regensburg, and Schönberg; finally arrives at Flossenbürg; executed on April 9 with Oster, Sack, Canaris, Strünck, and Gehre; von Dohnanyi executed in Sachsenhausen; Klaus Bonhoeffer and Rüdiger Schleicher executed two weeks later in Lehrterstrasse 3 prison; parents learn of his death in July

Appendix

Within a decade after Eberhard Bethge began to release the letters and writings of Dietrich Bonhoeffer, scholars began to engage his legacy and utilize his insights. Individuals began to pick up Bonhoeffer's theology, and doctoral dissertations began to appear (Hanfried Müller in 1956 and John Godsey in 1960). Within two decades, collegial groups of interested persons began meeting and joining efforts to make the legacy of Bonhoeffer more available. In 1970 the International Bonhoeffer Committee for Archive and Research was founded in Germany. Later renamed the International Bonhoeffer Society, there are now six sections: German, English, Polish, Dutch, Japanese, and Brazilian. Since the society's inception, several hundred scholars and interested laity from many countries have gathered every four years to share papers, projects, and conversation at the international congresses:

1. 1971—Kaiserswerth, West Germany

2. 1976—Geneva, Switzerland
   "The Work and Influence of Dietrich Bonhoeffer"

3. 1980—Oxford, England
   "Bonhoeffer and the Church in the Modern World"

4. 1984—Hirschluch, East Germany
   "Christian Freedom: The Struggle of Church & Culture"

5. 1988—Amsterdam, the Netherlands
   "Bonhoeffer's Ethical Legacy"

6. 1992—New York, U.S.A.
   "Responsibility in a New World"

7. 1996—Capetown, South Africa
   "Are We Still of Any Use? Bonhoeffer for a New Day"

8. 2000 Berlin, Germany
   "Religion and the Shape of Christianity in the 21st Century"
9. 2004 Rome, Italy
   "Dietrich Bonhoeffer and Christian Humanism"
10. 2008 Prague, Czech Republic
    "Dietrich Bonhoeffer's Theology in Today's World: A Way Between Fundamentalism and Secularism?
11. 2012 Sigtuna, Sweden
    "A Spoke in the Wheel: Reconsidering the Political in Bonhoeffer's Theology"

While the German Section of the Bonhoeffer Society meets several times each year and publishes a *Rundbrief*, the English Language Section meets annually in conjunction with the American Academy of Religion, and it issues a newsletter three times per year. The most significant project of the English Language Section has been to bring the *Dietrich Bonhoeffer Werke* (Chr. Kaiser/Gütersloher Verlagshaus) into English, a project to be completed in 2012.

In 1987 the retirement home of Karl and Paula Bonhoeffer (43 Marienbürger Allee, Berlin, Charlottenburg) was renovated and became a "place of memorial and encounter." The Bonhoeffer Haus has a permanent display of panels detailing the family's life from 1935 to 1945, including information about how the Bonhoeffer family was involved in the conspiracy to assassinate Hitler. Visitors are welcome year round, and tours of significant places around Berlin related to the Bonhoeffer legacy are arranged through the Haus. If there were a physical center or gathering place of the International Bonhoeffer Society, it would be the Bonhoeffer Haus in Berlin.

The International Bonhoeffer Society, while composed primarily of academics involved in research and writing about the legacy of Dietrich Bonhoeffer, invites pastors and laity to be part of their activities. The spirit of Dietrich Bonhoeffer, with that of Eberhard and Renate Bethge, continues to enrich the gatherings of the Bonhoeffer Society.

Acknowledgments

I want to thank those who over the years have inspired me and those whose present support makes possible my ongoing work on the legacy of Dietrich Bonhoeffer.

It was as a high school student in Muskegon, Michigan, that I first heard the name Dietrich Bonhoeffer. The pastor of Our Savior's Lutheran Church, my home congregation, was Reverend Lawrence C. Pratt Jr., and I distinctly remember him quoting from Bonhoeffer's *Ethics* in a sermon. Those were the turbulent 1960s, and in our multi-racial community I remember his words as being prophetic and profound. I could sense that an authentic connection was being made between the witness of Dietrich Bonhoeffer, the particular social setting of Muskegon, and our congregation's faith life. It was Pastor Pratt's bold proclamation of the Christ-reality referred to in Bonhoeffer's *Ethics* that, in part, occasioned his premature dismissal as pastor, as our all-white congregation struggled with the issue of race relations. It is to Larry (and his wife, Nancy, and their children Julie, Randy, Jane, Erik, and Kirsten, who shared with him the "cost of discipleship") that this book about, and my journey with, Dietrich Bonhoeffer is dedicated.

It is almost a litany, yet a litany grounded in reality, when most who write about Dietrich Bonhoeffer offer their thanks to Eberhard and Renate Bethge. Our gratitude to the Bethges lies beyond their gift of Bonhoeffer's theological legacy, which they preserved and passed on; for five decades they shared their knowledge and their humanity with the world, often traveling thousands of miles and getting very little sleep. I, like many others, was privileged to know them for over twenty years and call them friends. Eberhard died in 2000, and Renate lives on in their home in Villiprot. In addition to the Bethges, other family and friends of Bonhoeffer graciously shared with me significant things about their relationship and experiences with Dietrich, conversations which transformed my academic work into a rich life experience: Maria von Wedemeyer-Weller; Susanne, Walter and Andreas Dreß; Sabine, Gerhard, and Marianne Leibholz; Emmi Bonhoeffer; Werner and Dita Koch; Winfried Maechler; Albrecht Schönherr; Wolf-Dieter and Friederike Zimmermann; Paul and Marion Lehmann.

From members of the International Bonhoeffer Society I have benefited in ways great and small. Beginning with my initial enrollment in the society in 1975, through many national and international conferences, then as editor of the society's newsletter and finally serving as president from 2006-2009, I have been blessed with the conviviality and common sense, the wisdom and wit, that characterizes every gathering of that group. Especially to Pat Kelley, Michael Lukens, Geffrey Kelly, Martin Rumscheidt, Gaylon Barker, and Clifford Green, all impeccable scholars and loyal friends, I wish to express my gratitude. In my first book, *Anxious Souls Will Ask: The Christ-centered Spirituality of Dietrich Bonhoeffer* (Wm. B. Eerdmans Publishing Company, 2005), I indicated other members of the society who have journeyed with me since 1975, and for whom I am most grateful. Dr. James Burtness, my professor and thesis advisor at Luther Seminary, with his wife, Delores, were faithful and supportive all along the way, as was Dr. James Hofrenning, with whom I first studied Bonhoeffer at Concordia College in 1970. The following friends have all been conversation partners and enriched my life and theology beyond description: Chaplain Walter Pitt, my clinical pastoral education supervisor; Dr. Paul Sponheim, my systematic theology professor at Luther Seminary; Pastors Mark Molldrem, Ron Prasek, Erik Saxvik, Carol Solovitz, Michael Hayes, Roger Herfindahl, Anders Jonaker,

Gottfried Brezger, Lon Larson, Lloyd Ziebarth, Rabbi Barry Cytron, Imam Rashed Ferdous; the Burnsville Police Chaplains; Dan and Chris Rice, Duane and Karen Tangen, Randy and Christine Roen, Dan and Jill Cassada, Glenn Strand and Linda Kelsey, Kip and Deb Clayton, Jeff and Marcia Stavenger, Gary and Lee Blount, Jack and Cleo Young, Mark and Laurie Hintermeyer, Jerry and Marilyn Underwood, Jerry and Bonita Johnson, Bob and Mary McCoy; David Nimmer, Vince Schultz, Todd Bol, and David Beck. I often measure the fullness of my life by these persons I call friends.

It is in the context of parish ministry, now at Grace Lutheran Church of Apple Valley, Minnesota, that this book was written. To the staff and members of Grace I wish to express my thanks, as together we seek to "make the reality of Jesus Christ real." To Pastor Therese Helker, my colleague in ministry at Grace who is my daily theological conversation partner and one who carefully read this manuscript and offered helpful suggestions, I here express my sincere appreciation and deepest respect. To Leonard Flachman and Karen Walhof at Lutheran University Press; to Dr. Albert Anderson, the editor of this series; and to Dr. Martin Marty, who graciously agreed to write a foreword, I offer my sincere thanks.

Finally, it is Patty, my wife, who tops the list of people in my life who provide the most loving and supportive presence this side of heaven and who consistently reminds me of God's unconditional love; we have been graced with sixteen years of marital "life together" in all its fullness. To my parents of blessed memory, Walter and Beatrice, I here express my deepest gratitude. Our children and grandchildren continue to make us smile and remind us of God's desire for the kingdom to go on for another generation: Sari, Jon, Cole; Bryan, Cheri, Quinn; Maren, Jason, Dylan, Soren; Jodee, Tom, Addison, Tyler; Kayla and Alan. From my sister, Ann, and my cousins, Don, Chuck (Ruth Ann), and Mary (Mike), I have learned the importance of family and a love of humor.

Bibliography

For those desiring to study the Bonhoeffer legacy in greater depth, Eberhard Bethge's monumental biography of 1967 (in English, 1970), *Dietrich Bonhoeffer: Theologian, Christian, Contemporary,* which was retranslated and edited in 2000 by Victoria Barnett (Fortress Press), remains the definitive book about Bonhoeffer's life and legacy. An excellent, smaller biography, entitled *Dietrich Bonhoeffer 1906-45* (London: Continuum Imprint, 2010), was recently completed by Ferdinand Schlingensiepen, whose father was involved in the Confessing Church with Bonhoeffer. To dig even deeper, one would need to invest in the recently completed *Dietrich Bonhoeffer Works* by Fortress Press. This critical edition of sixteen volumes, which is a translation of the German *Dietrich Bonhoeffer Werke* (Christian Kaiser/Gütersloher Verlagshaus, Munich), includes virtually all of Bonhoeffer's extant writings, letters and lectures, with editorial comments from an international team of scholars. Two primary resources including more personal remembrances are *The Bonhoeffers: Portrait of a Family* (Chicago: Covenant Press, 1994) by Bonhoeffer's twin sister, Sabine, and *I Knew Dietrich Bonhoeffer* (New York: Harper and Row, 1966), edited by Bonhoeffer's student, Wolf-Dieter Zimmermann and R. Gregor Smith; the later includes reflections by thirty-five friends and family. Any persons interested in a representative yet smaller selection of Bonhoeffer's writings should secure *A Testament to Freedom: The Essential Writings of Dietrich Bonhoeffer* (Harper and Row, 1998), assembled by Bonhoeffer scholars Geffrey B. Kelly and F. Burton Nelson.

Bonhoeffer by Journey Films (Martin Doblmeier, director, 2006) and *Memories and Perspectives* by Trinity Films (Bainbridge Boelhke, director, 1983) remain outstanding documentaries on the life of Bonhoeffer, including numerous interviews with Bonhoeffer's family, friends, and students.

Primary Sources

Bonhoeffer, Dietrich. *Dietrich Bonhoeffer Works*, English edition (DBWE), eds. Wayne W. Floyd Jr., Victoria J. Barnett, and Barbara Wojhoski (Minneapolis: Fortress Press). These volumes are the critical, scholarly editions of the sixteen-volume *Dietrich Bonhoeffer Werke*, Chr. Kaiser/Gütersloher Verlagshaus.

Volume I, *Sanctorum Communio: A Theological Study of the Sociology of the Church*, tr. Reinhard Krauß and Nancy Lukens, ed. Clifford J. Green (1998).

Volume II, *Act and Being: Transcendental Philosophy and Ontology in Systematic Theology*, tr. H. Martin Rumscheidt, ed. Wayne W. Floyd Jr. (1996).

Volume III, *Creation and Fall: A Theological Exposition of Genesis 1-3*, tr. Douglas S. Bax, ed. John W. de Gruchy (1997).

Volume IV, *Discipleship*, tr. Barbara Green and Reinhard Krauß, ed. Geffrey B. Kelly and John D. Godsey (2001).

Volume V, *Life Together and The Prayerbook of the Bible: An Introduction to the Psalms*, tr. Daniel W. Bloesch and James H. Burtness, ed. Geffrey B. Kelly (1996).

Volume VI, *Ethics*, tr. Reinhard Krause, Charles C. West, and Douglas W. Stott, ed. Clifford J. Green (2005).

Volume VII, *Fiction from Tegel Prison*, tr. Nancy Lukens, ed. Clifford J. Green (1999).

Volume VIII, *Letters and Papers from Prison*, tr. Isobel Best, Lisa E. Dahill, Reinhard Krauß, Nancy Lukens, and H. Martin Rumscheidt, ed. John W. de Gruchy (2010).

Volume IX, *The Young Bonhoeffer, 1918-27*, tr. Mary Nebelsick and Douglas W. Stott, ed. Paul Duane Matheny, Clifford J. Green, and Marshall D. Johnson (2003).

Volume X, *Barcelona, Berlin, New York, 1928-1931*, tr. Douglas W. Stott, ed. Clifford J. Green (2008).

Volume XI, *Ecumenical, Academic and Pastoral Work 1931-1932*, tr. Nick Humphrey, Marion Pauck, and Anne Schmitt-Lange, ed. Michael B. Lukens and Mark S. Brocker (2012).

Volume XII, *Berlin 1932-1933*, tr. Isobel Best and David Higgins, ed. Larry Rasmussen (2009).

Volume XIII, *London, 1933-1935*, tr. Isobel Best and Douglas W. Stott, ed. Keith Clements (2007).

Volume XIV, *Theological Education at Finkenwalde 1935-1937*, tr. Douglas W. Stott, ed. Gaylon Barker and Stephen Plant (2012).

Volume XV, *Theological Education Underground 1937-1940*, tr. Victoria J. Barnett, Claudia Bergmann-Moore, and Peter Frick, ed. Victoria J. Barnett (2011).

Volume XVI, *Conspiracy and Imprisonment, 1940-1945*, tr. Lisa E. Dahill and Douglas W. Stott, ed. Mark S. Brocker (2006).

International Bibliography on Dietrich Bonhoeffer, ed. Ernst Feil (München: Chr.Kaiser Verlag, 1998). Annual updates are listed in the newsletter of the International Bonhoeffer Society, English Language Section.

Dietrich Bonhoeffer Jahrbuch (München: Chr. Kaiser/Gütersloher Verlagshaus. 2003/2005-2006). This series makes available all primary materials directly related to the Bonhoeffer legacy that have surfaced since the publication of the *Dietrich Bonhoeffer Werke*.

The Burke Library of Union Theological Seminary (New York City) is the depository for nearly all published and unpublished works by and about Dietrich Bonhoeffer in the English-speaking world.

Secondary Resources

Bethge, Eberhard. *Dietrich Bonhoeffer: A Biography*, rev. and ed. Victoria J. Barnett (Minneapolis: Fortress Press, 2000).

Bethge, Eberhard, ed. *Dietrich Bonhoeffer Werke*. (München: Chr. Kaiser/ Gütersloher Verlagshaus).

Bethge, Eberhard. *Nachlass Dietrich Bonhoeffer: Ein Verzeichnis*, ed. D. Meyer, Archiv – Sammlung – Bibliothek (München: Chr. Kaiser Verlag, 1987).

Bethge, Eberhard. *Costly Grace: An Illustrated Introduction to Dietrich Bonhoeffer* (San Francisco: Harper & Row, 1979).

Bethge, Eberhard. *Bonhoeffer: Exile and Martyr* (New York: The Seabury Press, 1975).

Bethge, Renate and Christian Gremmels, eds. *Bonhoeffer: A Life in Pictures* (Minneapolis: Fortress Press, 1986).

Bethge, Renate. "Bonhoeffer and the Role of Women," *Reflections on Bonhoeffer: Essays in Honor of F. Burton Nelson* (Chicago: Covenant Publications, 1999).

Barker, Gaylon H. *Cross of Reality: The Role of Luther's Theologia Crucis in the Development of Dietrich Bonhoeffer's Christology*, Sixth International Bonhoeffer Congress, New York (1992).

Barnett, Victoria J., ed. *Dietrich Bonhoeffer: A Biography* (Minneapolis: Fortress Press, 2000).

Barnett, Victoria. *For the Soul of the People: Protestant Protest Against Hitler* (New York: Oxford University Press, 1992).

Bartz, Paul. *I Am Bonhoeffer: A Credible Life* (Minneapolis: Fortress Press, 2008).

Berryhill, Elizabeth. *The Cup of Trembling: A Play in Two Acts*, suggested by and with material derived from the life of Dietrich Bonhoeffer (New York: Seabury, 1958).

Blount, Gary. "Creaking in the Beams, Dietrich Bonhoeffer, Christianity and the Third Reich." *Spectrum*, Summer 2002, Volume 30, Issue no. 3: 35-41.

Bosanquet, Mary. *The Life and Death of Dietrich Bonhoeffer* (New York: Harper and Row, 1968).

Brezger, Gottfried. *"Wie kann Christus der Herr auch der Religionslosen werden?"* Inklusivgewendete Christologie bei Dietrich Bonhoeffer, Tenth International Bonhoeffer Congress, Prague (2008).

Brocker, Mark. "The Community of God, Jesus Christ and Responsibility: The Responsible Person and the Responsible Community in the Ethics of Dietrich Bonhoeffer," Ph.D. dissertation (Chicago: The University of Chicago, 1996).

Burnell, Joel. *Poetry, Providence, and Patriotism: Polish Messianism in Dialogue with Dietrich Bonhoeffer* (Eugene, Oregon: Pickwick Publications, 2009).

Burtness, James H. *Shaping the Future* (Philadelphia: Fortress Press, 1985).

Burtness, James H. *Consequences* (Minneapolis: Fortress Press, 1999).

Carter, Guy Christian. "Confession from Bethel, August 1933—Enduring Witness," Ph.D. dissertation (Milwaukee: Marquette University, 1986).

Chandler, Andrew. "The Quest for the Historical Dietrich Bonhoeffer," *The Journal of Ecclesiastical History 54*, no. 1 (2003): 89-96.

Chapman, Clark G. Jr. "Bonhoeffer and Liberation Theology," *Ethical Responsibility: Bonhoeffer's Legacy to the Churches* (Godsey/Kelly).

Clements, Keith. *Bonhoeffer in Britain* (London: Churches Together in Britain and Ireland, 2006).

Clements, Keith. *Bonhoeffer* (London: SPCK, 2010).

Conway, John. "Bonhoeffer's Last Writings from Prison," *CRUX* (Vancouver: Regent College) Fall 2006, 42.3: 2-9.

Dahill, Lisa. "Reading from the Underside of Selfhood: Bonhoeffer and Spiritual Formation," *Princeton Theological Monograph Series 95* (Eugene, Oregon: Pickwick Publications, 2009).

de Gruchy, John W. *Daring, Trusting Spirit: Bonhoeffer's Friend Eberhard Bethge* (Minneapolis: Fortress Press, 2005).

de Gruchy, John W. *Bonhoeffer and South Africa: Theology in Dialogue* (Grand Rapids: Wm. B. Eerdmans Publishing Co., 1984).

de Gruchy, John W. *The Cambridge Companion to Dietrich Bonhoeffer* (Cambridge: Cambridge University Press, 1999).

De Lange, Frits. *Waiting for the Word* (Grand Rapids: Wm. B. Eerdmans Publishing Co., 2000).

Dramm, Sabine. *Dietrich Bonhoeffer and the Resistance* (Minneapolis: Fortress Press, 2009).

Dumas, André. *Dietrich Bonhoeffer: Theologian of Reality* (New York: The Macmillan Co., 1971).

Elshtain, Jean Bethke. *Who Are We?* (Grand Rapids: Wm. B. Eerdmans, 2000).

Feil, Ernst. *The Theology of Dietrich Bonhoeffer* (Philadelphia: Fortress Press, 1985).

Floyd, Wayne W. Jr. *The Wisdom and Witness of Dietrich Bonhoeffer* (Minneapolis: Fortress Press, 2000).

Floyd, Wayne W. Jr. T*heology and the Practice of Responsibility: Essays on Dietrich Bonhoeffer,* ed. with Charles Marsh (Valley Forge, Pennsylvania: Trinity Press International, 1994).

Frick, Peter. *Bonhoeffer's Intellectual Formation: Theology and Philosophy in His Thought,* Religion in Philosophy & Theology 29 (Tübingen: Mohr Siebeck, 2008).

Gallas, Alberto. *"La centralita del Dio inutile,"* Bonhoeffer, Dietrich: *Resistenza e Resa. Lettere e scritti dal carcere* (Milano, 1988): 5-46.

Giardina, Denise. *Saints and Villains* (New York: Faucet, 1998).

Gilbert, Douglas and Martin J. Bailey. *The Steps of Bonhoeffer: A Pictoral Album* (Philadelphia: Pilgrim Press, 1969).

Glazener, Mary. *The Cup of Wrath* (Macon, Georgia: Smyth & Helwys, 1992 and 1996).

Godsey, John D. *The Theology of Dietrich Bonhoeffer* (Philadelphia: Westminster Press, 1960).

Godsey, John D. *Preface to Bonhoeffer: The Man and Two of His Shorter Writings* (Philadelphia: Fortress Press, 1965).

Godsey, John D. *Ethical Responsibility: Bonhoeffer's Legacy to the Churches,* ed. with Geffrey B. Kelly (New York: Edwin Mellen Press, 1981).

Green, Clifford J. *Bonhoeffer: A Theology of Sociality* (Grand Rapids: Wm. B. Eerdmans Publishing Co., 1999).

Greenberg, Irving. "Partnership in the Covenant: Bonhoeffer and the Future of Jewish-Christian Relations," Conference paper at the Sixth International Bonhoeffer Congress, New York (1992).

Hale, Lori Brandt. "From Loving Enemies to Acting Responsibly: Forgiveness in the Life and Theology of Dietrich Bonhoeffer," *Word and World,* 27, no. 1 (2007): 79-87.

Hale, Lori Brandt. *Bonhoeffer for Armchair Theologians,* with Stephen Haynes (Louisville: Westminster John Knox Press, 2009).

Harvey, Barry H. "A Post-Critical Approach to a 'Religionless Christianity,'" *Union Seminary Quarterly Review,* 46 (1992): 39-58.

Hauerwas, Stanley. *Performing the Faith: Bonhoeffer and the Practice of Non-Violence* (Grand Rapids: Brazos, 2004).

Haynes, Stephen R. *The Bonhoeffer Phenomenon: Portraits of a Protestant Saint* (Minneapolis: Fortress Press, 2004).

Haynes, Stephen R. *The Bonhoeffer Legacy: Post-Holocaust Perspectives* (Minneapolis: Fortress Press, 2006).

Hopper, David H. *A Dissent on Bonhoeffer* (Philadelphia: Westminster Press, 1975).

Huber, Wolfgang. *"Wer ist Christus für uns? Bonhoeffers Bedeutung für die Zukunft der Christenheit,"* Evangelische Kommentare, 19 (1986): 191-194.

Hüneke, Martin. *"Christliche Erfahrung bei Dietrich Bonhoeffer. Begegnung mit dem 'fremden Wort Gottes,'"* Internationale Katholische Zeitschrift Communio, 25 (1996): 240-252.

Huntemann, Georg. *The Other Bonhoeffer: An Evangelical Reassessment of Dietrich Bonhoeffer* (Grand Rapids: Baker Publishing, 1993).

Kelley, James P. "Bonhoeffer Studies in English: How Theologians Become Popular," *Lexington Theological Quarterly,* 3:1 (1968): 12-19.

Kelly, Geffrey B. *Liberating Faith: Bonhoeffer's Message for Today* (Minneapolis: Augsburg Publishing House, 1984).

Kelly, Geffrey B. *A Testament to Freedom: The Essential Writings of Dietrich Bonhoeffer* with F. Burton Nelson, eds. (San Francisco: Harper San Francisco, 1990).

Kelly, Geffrey B. *The Cost of Moral Leadership: The Spirituality of Dietrich Bonhoeffer* with F. Burton Nelson, eds. (Grand Rapids: Wm. B. Eerdmans Publishing Co., 2002).

Kelly, Geffrey B. *Reading Bonhoeffer: A Guide to His Spiritual Classics and Selected Writings on Peace* (Oregon: Cascade Books, 2008).

Klassen, A. J., ed. *A Bonhoeffer Legacy: Essays in Understanding* (Grand Rapids: Wm. B. Eerdmans Publishing Co., 1981).

Koch, Werner. "The Acceptance of Guilt by Dietrich Bonhoeffer," Paper presented at the Fifth International Bonhoeffer Congress, Amsterdam (New York: Burke Library, Union Theological Seminary, 1988).

Lawrence, Joel. *Bonhoeffer: A Guide for the Perplexed* (New York: T&T Clark International, 2010).

Lehmann, Paul. "Commentary: Dietrich Bonhoeffer in America," *Religion in Life*, 30:4 (1961): 616-618.

Leibholz, Sabine. *The Bonhoeffers: Portrait of a Family* (Chicago: Covenant Press, 1994).

Ligus, Ján. *"Theologicky, ekumenicky a svedeckyodkaz Dietricha Bonhoeffera," Theologická revue, Nábozenskydvoumesicnik Husitsketeologickefakulty University Karolvy v Praze* (1995) 1: 13-16; 2: 19-23.

Lovin, Robin. *Christian Faith and Public Choices: The Social Ethics of Barth, Brunner and Bonhoeffer* (Philadelphia: Fortress Press, 1984).

Maechler, Winfried. *"Vom Pazifistenzum Widerstandskämpfer: Bonhoeffers Kampf für die Entrechteten," Die Mündige Welt* (München: Chr. Kaiser Verlag, 1955), 89-95.

Marsh, Charles. *Reclaiming Dietrich Bonhoeffer* (Oxford: Oxford University Press, 1994).

Marty, Martin. ed. *The Place of Bonhoeffer: Problems and Possibilities in His Thought* (New York: Associated Press, 1962).

Marty, Martin. *Dietrich Bonhoeffer's Letters and Papers from Prison: A Biography* (Princeton: Princeton University Press, 2011).

Matthews, John W. *Anxious Souls Will Ask: The Christ-centered Spirituality of Dietrich Bonhoeffer* (Grand Rapids: Wm. B. Eerdmans Publishing Co., 2005).

Matthews, John W. "Responsible Sharing of the Mystery of Christian Faith: *Disciplina Arcani* in the Life and Theology of Dietrich Bonhoeffer," *Dialog*, Winter 1986.

Matthews, John W. "Dietrich Bonhoeffer—Pastor and Theologian of Word and World," *Word & World*, Volume 26, Summer 2006.

McBride, Jennifer M. and Willis Jenkins, eds. *Bonhoeffer and King: Their Legacies and Import for Christian Social Thought* (Minneapolis: Fortress Press, 2010).

Metaxas, Eric. *Bonhoeffer: Pastor, Martyr, Prophet, Spy* (Nashville: Thomas Nelson, 2010).

Moltmann, Jürgen and Jürgen Weissbach. *Two Studies in the Theology of Dietrich Bonhoeffer* (New York: Scribner's Sons, 1967).

Moses, John A. "Bonhoeffer's Germany: The Political Context," *The Cambridge Companion to Dietrich Bonhoeffer*, ed. John W. de Gruchy (1999): 3-21.

Müller, Hanfried. *Von der Kirchezur Welt: EinBeitragzu der Beziehung des Wortes Gottes auf die Societas in Dietrich Bonhoeffers theologischer Entwicklung* (Hamburg-Bergstadt: Herbert Reich Evangelischer Verlag, 1961).

Murakami, Hiroshi. *Bonhoeffer und Japan, Festschristzum 80.Geburtstag Eberhard Bethges,* Bonhoeffer to Nihon (Tokio, 1989).

Nelson, F. Burton. *A Testament to Freedom: The Essential Writings of Dietrich Bonhoeffer,* ed. with Geffrey B. Kelly (San Francisco: HarperSanFrancisco, 1990).

Nielsen, Kirsten Busch. *"Kirke, faelleskabetogteologien. Dietrich Bonhoeffersekklesiologi,"* Okumeniske Studier 3 (Frederiksberg, 1989).

Nielsen, Kirsten Busch. *Mysteries in the Theology of Dietrich Bonhoeffer: A Copenhagen Bonhoeffer Symposium,* ed. with Ulrich Nissen and Christiane Tietz (Göttingen: Vandenhoeck & Ruprecht, 2007).

Ott, Heinrich. *Reality and Faith: The Theological Legacy of Dietrich Bonhoeffer* (Philadelphia: Fortress Press, 1972).

Pangritz, Andreas. *Karl Barth in the Theology of Dietrich Bonhoeffer* (Grand Rapids: Wm. B. Eerdmans Publishing Co., 2000).

Peck, William J., ed. *New Studies in Bonhoeffer's Ethics* (Lewiston/Queenstown: Edwin Mellen Press, 1987).

Pejsa, Jane. *Matriarch of Conspiracy: Ruth von Kleist, 1867-1945* (Minneapolis: Kenwood Publishing. 1991).

Pfeifer, Hans. "Dietrich Bonhoeffers *'Interims' Ethik."* Paper presented at the Tenth International Bonhoeffer Congress, Prague (2008).

Phillips, John. *Christ for Us in the Theology of Dietrich Bonhoeffer* (New York: Harper Row Publishers, 1967).

Plant, Stephen. *Bonhoeffer* (London: Continuum Imprint, 2004).

Pugh, Jeffrey C. *Religionless Christianity: Dietrich Bonhoeffer in Troubled Times* (London: Continuum Imprint, 2008).

Rasmussen, Larry L. *Dietrich Bonhoeffer: Reality and Resistance* (Nashville: Abingdon, 1972).

Rasmussen, Larry L. *Dietrich Bonhoeffer: His Significance for North Americans,* with Renate Bethge (Minneapolis: Fortress Press, 1990).

Raum, Elizabeth. *Dietrich Bonhoeffer: Called By God* (New York: Continuum International Group, 2002).

Roberts, J. Deotis. *Bonhoeffer & King* (Louisville: Westminster John Knox Press, 2005).

Robertson, Edwin. *Dietrich Bonhoeffer* (Richmond: John Knox, 1967).

Robinson, John A.T. *Honest to God* (Philadelphia: Westminster Press, 1963).

Rubenstein, Richard L. "Dietrich Bonhoeffer and Pope Pius XII," Paper presented on the thirtieth anniversary of the Annual Scholars' Conference on the Holocaust and the Churches (2005).

Rumscheidt, H. Martin. "The View from Below: Dietrich Bonhoeffer's Reflections and Actions on Racism," *Toronto Journal of Theology* 24 (2008): 63-72.

Schliesser, Christine. *Everyone Who Acts Responsibly Becomes Guilty: Bonhoeffer's Concept of Accepting Guilt* (Louisville/London: Westminster John Knox, 2008).

Schlingensiepen, Ferdinand. *Dietrich Bonhoeffer 1906-45* (London: Continuum Imprint, 2010).

Schönherr, Albrecht. "Dietrich Bonhoeffer: The Message of a Life," *Christian Century* 102 (November 27, 1985): 1090-94.

Sensel, Charles. "A Periscope for Bonhoeffer's Theology," *Reflections on Bonhoeffer: Essays in Honor of F. Burton Nelson* (Chicago: Covenant Publications, 1999).

Sherman, Franklin. "The Problem of a Trinitarian Social Ethic: A Study in the Theological Foundations of Christian Social Ethics, with Special Reference to Werner Elert and Dietrich Bonhoeffer," PhD. dissertation (Chicago: University of Chicago, 1961).

Slane, Craig J. *Bonhoeffer as Martyr: Social Responsibility and Modern Christian Commitment* (Grand Rapids: Brazos, 2004).

Sorum, Jonathan. "God's Humanity in an Inhuman World: The Offer of a Truly Human Life in Bonhoeffer's Discipleship," Paper presented at the Ninth International Bonhoeffer Congress, Rome (2004).

Staggs, Alvin D. *A View from the Underside: The Legacy of Dietrich Bonhoeffer* (Macon, Georgia: Smyth & Helwys, 2002).

Stassen, Glenn H. *Living the Sermon on the Mount: A Practical Hope for Grace and Deliverance* (San Francisco: Jossey-Bass, 2006).

Tietz, Christiane. *Dietrich Bonhoeffer's Theology Today: A Way between Fundamentalism and Secularism?* ed. with Stephen Plant (Gütersloh: Gütersloher Verlagshaus, 2009).

Tödt, Heinz Eduard. *Authentic Faith: Bonhoeffer's Theological Ethics in Context* (Grand Rapids: Wm. B. Eerdmans Publishing Co., 2007).

Tödt, Ilse. "Paradoxical Obedience: Dietrich Bonhoeffer's Theological Ethics, 1933-1945," *Lutheran Theological Journal* 35.1 (2001): 3-16.

West, Charles. *The Power to be Human: Toward a Secular Theology* (New York: Macmillan Press, 1970).

Williams, Rowan. "Bonhoeffer and European Identity," "Bearing Responsibility for Others," ed. Joel Burnell. Papers presented at the 100th anniversary of Dietrich Bonhoeffer's birth in Wroclaw, Poland (February 2006), 157-158

Wind, Renate. *A Spoke in the Wheel: The Life of Dietrich Bonhoeffer* (Grand Rapids: Wm. B. Eerdmans Publishing Co., 1991).

Wise, Stephen, A. "Why Isn't Bonhoeffer Honored at Yad Vashem?" *Christian Century*, 115 (February 25, 1998), 202-04.

Woelfel, James. W. *Bonhoeffer's Theology: Classical and Revolutionary* (Nashville/ New York: Abingdon Press, 1970).

Wüstenberg, Ralf K. *A Theology of Life: Dietrich Bonhoeffer's Religionless Christianity* (Grand Rapids: Wm. B. Eerdmans Publishing Co., 1998).

Young, Josiah U. III. *No Difference in the Fare: Dietrich Bonhoeffer and the Problem of Racism* (Grand Rapids: Wm. B. Eerdmans Publishing Co., 1998).

Zerner, Ruth. "Dietrich Bonhoeffer's American Experiences: People, Letters, and Papers from Union Seminary," *Union Seminary Quarterly Review*. 31/4 (1976): 261-282.

Zimmermann, Jens and Brian Gregor, eds. *Bonhoeffer and Continental Thought* (Bloomington, Indiana: Indiana University Press, 2009).

Zimmermann, Wolf-Dieter with R. Gregor Smith, eds. *I Knew Dietrich Bonhoeffer* (New York: Harper and Row Publishers, 1966).

Endnotes

1   Eberhard Bethge, *Dietrich Bonhoeffer: A Biography*, ed. Victoria J. Barnett (Minneapolis: Fortress Press, 2000), 105. Hereafter referred to as DB.

2   DB, 655.

3   *Dietrich Bonhoeffer Works*, eds. Victoria J. Barnett and Barbara Wojhoski. (Minneapolis: Fortress Press, 1996). Hereafter referred to as DBWE.

4   *I Knew Dietrich Bonhoeffer: Reminiscences of Friends,* eds. Wolf-Dieter Zimmermann and Ronald Gregor Smith (New York: Harper and Row Publishers, 1966), 232.

5   Heinrich Ott, *Reality and Faith: The Theological Legacy of Dietrich Bonhoeffer* (Philadelphia: Fortress Press, 1972), 368-69.

6   Ernst Feil, *The Theology of Dietrich Bonhoeffer* (Philadelphia: Fortress Press, 1985), 95-96.

7   André Dumas, *Dietrich Bonhoeffer: Theologian of Reality* (New York: Macmillan, 1971), 215.

8   DB, 219.

9   DBWE 12, 299.

10 Ibid., 300.

11 Ibid., 302 ff.

12 Ibid., 310.

13 Ibid., 311.

14 Ibid., 314.

15 John A. Phillips, *Christ for Us in the Theology of Dietrich Bonhoeffer* (New York: Harper & Row, Publishers, 1967), 80.

16 Ibid.

17 DBWE 12, 316-317.

18 Ibid., 319.

19 Ibid., 318.

20 Ibid., 321.

21 Ibid., 323.

22 Ibid., 324.

23 Ibid.

24 Ibid., 325-26.

25 Ibid., 327.

26 Ibid., 360.

27 Ibid., 300.

28 DBWE 8, 373.

29 John W. Matthews, "Responsible Sharing of the Mystery of Christian Faith": *Disciplina Arcani* in the Life and Theology of Dietrich Bonhoeffer," *Dialog* 25, no. 1 (1986): 19-25.

30 "The Barmen Declaration," May 1934.

31 The Bible Bonhoeffer used for personal meditation was originally his brother Walter's. After Walter's death in 1918, Dietrich's mother gave it to him, and it was this Bible that he took with him to Tegel prison.

32 DBWE 8, 61.

33 Ibid., 139 (a quote of Leviticus 26:6).

34 Ibid., 213.

35 Ibid., 366, 367, 406, 448.

36 Ibid., 486.

37 Ibid.

38 DB, 927.

[39] Karl Barth, *Church Dogmatics IV-2* (Edinburgh: T. & T. Clark, 1960), 641.

[40] DBWE 1, 65, 80.

[41] Othmar Spann, *Gesellschaftslehre*, second edition (Leipzig, 1923).

[42] Clifford Green, *The Cambridge Companion to Dietrich Bonhoeffer*. ed. John deGruchy (Cambridge: Cambridge University Press, 1999), 124.

[43] Clifford J. Green, *Bonhoeffer: A Theology of Sociality* (Grand Rapids: Wm. B. Eerdmans Publishing Company, 1999).

[44] DB, 83.

[45] DBWE 1, 33.

[46] DBWE 5, 10.

[47] Ibid., 8.

[48] Ibid., 6.

[49] DBWE 1, 121, 141, 216.

[50] DBWE 5, 127.

[51] Ibid., 27, 29.

[52] Ibid., 29, 31.

[53] Ibid., 35-36, 38.

[54] Ibid., 38.

[55] Ibid., 55.

[56] Ibid., 83.

[57] Ibid., 98-100.

[58] Ibid., 108.

[59] Ibid., 117.

[60] Ibid., 113, 110.

[61] Ibid., 110.

[62] Ibid.

[63] Ibid., 111.

[64] Ibid., 112.

[65] Ibid., 113.

[66] Ibid., 114-115.

[67] Ibid., 118.

[68] Although *Discipleship* is the title of volume 4 of the DBWE (2001), closely adhering to the German title of 1937 (*Nachfolge*), most know this book as *The Cost of Discipleship*, an English title first used in 1948.

[69] DB, 36.

[70] DBWE 4, 43.

[71] Ibid., 43-44.

[72] Ibid., 45.

[73] Ibid., 53.

[74] Ibid., 50-51.

[75] Ibid., 51.

[76] Stephen R. Haynes and Lori Brandt Hale, *Bonhoeffer for Armchair Theologians* (Louisville: Westminster John Knox Press, 2009), 105.

[77] DBWE 4, 55.

[78] Ibid., 59.

[79] Ibid., 63-64.

[80] Ibid., 85, 87.

[81] Ibid., 59.

[82] Ibid., 89.

[83] Ibid., 100-110.

[84] Ibid.

[85] Ibid., 207-208.

[86] Ibid., 94-95.

[87] Ibid., 40, 91.

[88] Joel Lawrence, *Bonhoeffer: A Guide for the Perplexed* (New York: T&T Clark International, 2010), 84.

[89] DBWE 8, 486.

[90] Eberhard Bethge, "The Chicago Theological Seminary Register," volume LI, number 2, February 1961: 21.

[91] *A Bonhoeffer Legacy: Essays in Understanding*, ed. A.J. Klassen (Grand Rapids: Wm. B. Eerdmans Publishing Company, 1981), 165.

[92] DBWE 4, 32.

[93] Eberhard Bethge, "The Chicago Theological Seminary Register," volume LI, number 2, February 1961.

[94] James Patrick Kelley, "Revelation and the Secular in the Theology of

Dietrich Bonhoeffer," Ph.D. dissertation, May 1980, Yale University.

95 DBWE 8, 27.

96 DBWE 6, 47.

97 Ibid., 300.

98 Ibid., 299.

99 Ibid., 81.

100 The reason for rearranging portions of Bonhoeffer's *Ethics* as recently as 1998 is that research continued to surface new options about the dating of various chapters of his ethical writings. In an effort that resembled archeology, the paper and ink used by Bonhoeffer offered evidence for ordering the chapters chronologically.

101 DBWE 6, 74.

102 Ibid., 56, 58.

103 Ibid., 58.

104 Ibid., 62.

105 Ibid., 55, 65.

106 Ibid., 47, 50-51.

107 Ibid., 63.

108 Ibid., 257.

109 Ibid., 288.

110 DBWE 1, 121, 146, 155, 182.

111 DBWE 6, 259.

112 Ibid., 234.

113 DBWE 8, 486.

114 DBWE 6, 285.

115 Ibid., 287-288.

116 Ibid., 79.

117 Ferdinand Schlingensiepen. *Dietrich Bonhoeffer: 1906-1945* (New York: T&T Clark International), 251.

118 Larry Rasmussen, *Dietrich Bonhoeffer: Reality and Resistance* (Louisville: Westminster John Knox Press, 1972; republished in 2005).

119 DBWE 6, 146 ff.

120 Ibid., 155-157.

121 Ibid., 167.

122 Ibid., 163.

123 James Burtness, *Shaping the Future: The Ethics of Dietrich Bonhoeffer* (Philadelphia: Fortress Press, 1985), 7.

124 DBWE 7.

125 DBWE 8, 352.

126 Ibid., 571.

127 Ibid., 1, 2.

128 DBWE 8.

129 The first American edition was published in 1954 by Macmillan in New York, titled *Prisoner for God: Letters and Papers from Prison.*

130 *Dietrich Bonhoeffer Works, Volume 16: Conspiracy and Imprisonment 1940-1945* (Minneapolis: Fortress Press, 2006), 15.

131 Dietrich Bonhoeffer and Maria von Wedemeyer, *Love Letters from Cell 92: The Correspondence Between Dietrich Bonhoeffer and Maria von Wedemeyer 1943-1945.* (London: Harper Collins, 1994). By Maria's request, these personal letters were not made public until after her death; she died of cancer in 1977, in Boston.

132 Martin E. Marty, *The Place of Bonhoeffer: Problems and Possibilities in His Thought* (New York: Associated Press, 1962).

133 Martin E. Marty, *Dietrich Bonhoeffer's Letters and Papers from Prison: A Biography* (Princeton: Princeton University Press, 2011).

134 DBWE 8, 362-367.

135 Ibid., 372.

136 Ibid.

137 Ibid., 363.

138 Ibid., 372.

139 Ibid., 405-406.

140 DBWE 12, 324-327.

141 DBWE 8, 406.

142 The word *mündigkeit* refers to maturity, when people arrive at the age they are expected to act responsibly. This state of adulthood is contrasted with that of childhood, when young people are expected to depend on their parents and defer to those who are older. Bonhoeffer's observation is that religion had tended to encourage people to remain (religiously) dependent and immature.

143 Ibid., 406.

144 Ibid., 429.

145 Ibid., 428.

146 Ibid., 476 ff.

147 Ibid.

148 Ibid., 478-479.

149 Ibid., 479.

150 Ibid., 480.

151 Ibid., 486.

152 John W. de Gruchy, *Daring, Trusting Spirit: Bonhoeffer's Friend Eberhard Bethge* (Minneapolis: Fortress Press, 2005), 85.

153 DBWE 8, 486.

154 DBWE 8, 37.

155 Ibid., 499.

156 Ibid., 37.

157 Ibid., 40.

158 Ibid., 52.

159 Ibid., 513.

160 DBWE 1, 191.

161 For a very helpful introduction to this issue, see Stephen R. Haynes' *The Bonhoeffer Legacy: Post-Holocaust Perspective* (Minneapolis: Fortress Press, 2006).

162 Christian supercessionism is the idea that Christianity, as a scheme of salvation for all of humanity, renders the validity and mission of Israel/Jews/Judaism no longer necessary, meaning that the Christian message of God's grace in Jesus Christ supercedes all former covenants and actions of God.

163 "The Church and the Jewish Question" (April 1933). See DBWE 12, 361-370.

164 Spoken to the author by Rev. Richard Borgstrom.

165 Stephen A. Wise, the grandson of Rabbi Stephen S. Wise, has worked feverishly to document and then argue for Bonhoeffer's inclusion in the Avenue of the Righteous at Yad Vashem. Wise argues that Bonhoeffer meets the criterion of "assisting at least one Jew, at risk to his own life," regardless of what his theological convictions were. Wise's efforts have not proven successful yet, but his arguments and devotion to that cause can be referenced in *The Christian Century*, 25 February 1998, 202-204.

166 Craig J. Slane, *Bonhoeffer as Martyr: Social Responsibility and Modern Christian Commitment* (Grand Rapids: Brazos Press. 2003).

167 DB, 931.

168 See Andrew Chandler, ed., *The Terrible Alternative: Christian Martyrdom in the Twentieth Century* (London: Cassell, 1998).

169 Dahill, Lisa E., "Reading from the Underside of Selfhood: Bonhoeffer and Spiritual Formation," *Princeton Theological Monograph Series 95* (Eugene, Oregon: Pickwick Publications, 2009): 171.

170 Andras Csepregi, a Hungarian scholar, presented this paper, now archived at the Burke Library of Union Theological Seminary in New York City, at the 9th International Bonhoeffer Congress in Rome (June 2004).